how to hold a grudge

From Resentment to Contentment –
the Power of Grudges to Transform Your Life

SOPHIE HANNAH

HODDER

First published in Great Britain in 2018 by Hodder & Stoughton
An Hachette UK company

This paperback edition published in 2019

1

A CIP catalogue record for this title is
available from the British Library

Paperback ISBN 9781473695559

Typeset in Aldine 401 by Palimpsest Book Production Ltd, Falkirk, Stirlingshire

Printed and bound in Great Britain by Clays Ltd, Elcograf S.p.A.

Hodder & Stoughton policy is to use papers that are natural, renewable
and recyclable products and made from wood grown in sustainable forests.
The logging and manufacturing processes are expected to conform to the
environmental regulations of the country of origin.

Hodder & Stoughton Ltd
Carmelite House
50 Victoria Embankment
London EC4Y 0DZ

www.hodder.co.uk

Contents

Introduction

This book might never have happened if my sister and I had not had a conversation that went something like this:

ME: I'm thinking of writing a self-help book called *How to Be a Doormat* – one that, on the face of it, advocates being a pushover, and describes what will happen to you if you are one. The *real* aim, of course, will be to show that it's *not* a great idea to be a doormat. It'll be a reverse psychology self-help book.

HER: You definitely shouldn't write that book.

ME: Why not?

HER: Because you're not a doormat, or a pushover. Any book on the subject should be written by a true doormat.

ME: And . . . I'm not one?

HER: No.

ME: Oh. Then what am I?

(Don't I sound *so* much like a doormat at this point?
Asking to be told what I am? I mean, who does that?)

Presses rewind

ME: Oh. Then what am I?

HER: You're someone who holds grudges.

ME: Ha! Well, obviously. Who isn't? Everyone holds
         grudges.

HER: Not the way you do. You devote more care and
         attention to the collection, analysis and maintenance
         of grudges than anyone I've ever known.

ME: Hold on – I always give second chances, though. I
         never cut anyone out of my life, no matter what
         they've done. Remember Dillon from Indianapolis,
         who kept attacking me on Twitter? I ended up
         suggesting that he and I do an event together at a
         literary festival, where we could discuss in front of
         an audience whether I was okay or a horrendous
         person.

HER: Did that happen? I didn't know about that. Did
         you really suggest that?

ME: Yup.

HER: Well . . . that was fucking stupid of you. Are you
        seriously denying that you hold grudges?

ME: No, I definitely do, but . . . not in a bad way. I
        hold *good* grudges.

HER: Is there a difference?

ME: Of course.

HER: What is it?

ME: Is that a serious question? Do you honestly not
        know? Maybe I should write a book called *How to
        Hold a Grudge* – though there are probably dozens
        already. Let me look online . . .

Guess what? Before I wrote this one, no book on the specific
subject of grudges existed. Nobody, it seemed, had ever
undertaken a thorough analysis of grudges as a psychological
phenomenon, or suggested how we should handle and think
about them, or examined the role they play in our lives. Can
you believe it? I couldn't. Grudges are so universal, such an
important and fascinating part of human experience. They
inspire songs, movies, books, political careers and even architecture (see Chapter 5 for details!). We've all held a grudge,
tried to shake one off or discovered that someone we know
is holding one against us.

It was January 2016 when I had the above conversation

with my sister, and the world urgently needed a book on the subject of grudges. Since I was surrounded on all sides by lazyboneses who weren't showing any signs of producing that book, I decided to write it myself.

In these pages, you'll find everything you need to know about the many different types and themes of grudge, how to grade a grudge, the difference between a grudge and not-a-grudge (which isn't as obvious as it seems), when we should let a grudge go, how to manage your Grudge Budget (or Grudget), and how to honour your grudges and distil lessons from them that will turn you into a better, happier person, for your own good and for the sake of spreading good and limiting harm in the world. You will also find plenty of my grudge stories, and many sent in by other people. In nearly all of these, minor changes have been made to the details that don't matter. Dillon from Indianapolis, for example, might in real life be Garry from Helsinki. (He isn't, of course. I don't want to be sued by Garry from Helsinki either.) A niece might have been turned into a sister-in-law; a pet rabbit might have become a pet hamster; a story might be moved from Basingstoke to Boston or Barcelona. I will sometimes refer to people no longer in my life as if they are still around.

The opinions, advice and theories offered in this book, unless attributed to others, are mine and mine alone. I am not a psychotherapist and not a trained counsellor or mental health expert of any kind. I'm someone with forty-seven years of active and regular grudge-holding experience (remember: 'You devote more care and attention to the collection, analysis and maintenance of grudges than anyone I've ever known' – Sophie's sister) and a strong interest in the subject, and you are welcome to disagree with me about any

4

or all of it! I'd love to hear from you, whether you agree or disagree, and you can contact me via the 'Contact' button on the home page of my website: www.sophiehannah.com or at grudgescanbegood@gmail.com.

I asked two experienced therapists whom I admire and trust to read an early manuscript and send me their thoughts and responses. They are Helen Acton and Anne Grey, and I've included some of their insights in the text. You can find more information about Helen and Anne at the back of this book.

1

Grudges Can Be Great!

'People believe that in order to live a happy life that they enjoy, they have to be delusional and sugar-coat everything. They pretend that bad things aren't bad, that mean things aren't mean, that people are good for them who really aren't. It's better to be realistic, and find a way to cope with the negative stuff. Don't sugar-coat anything – recognise the problem and deal with it. People think that to forgive and forget is the healthiest thing. It's not.'

Phoebe Jones, age 16

Secretly we all hold grudges, but most of us probably think we shouldn't, and many of us deny that we do. To bear a grudge is too negative, right? Instead, we should forgive and move on?

Wrong.

Actually, it's not exactly wrong. It's kind of right, but in the wrong way. Confused? Then read on and you'll soon understand what I mean.

Of course it's essential to think positive if you want to live a happy life, but even more crucial is how you get to that positive. Denying your negative emotions and experiences in the hope that they will disappear from memory and leave you feeling and thinking exactly as you did before they happened will lead only to more pain, conflict and stress in the long term.

So what should you do instead? The short answer is: you should follow the Grudge-fold Path.

'What the hell does that mean?' I hear you ask. Read on and you will soon know. For the time being, though, I'll give you a different short answer (which is actually the same answer but expressed normally rather than in weird jargon I've invented): you should hold a grudge, and *then* forgive and move on, *while still holding your grudge*. Does that sound like a contradiction? The mission of this book is to explain why it's not, and to lay out in simple steps what it means to follow the Grudge-fold Path.

Am I seriously going to encourage you to hold grudges? Yes, I am. And I'm going to start by asking you to consider these questions: what if everyone who has ever told you, 'Don't hold grudges because it's bad for you and not very nice' was wrong? What if our grudges are good for us? What if they're the psychological equivalent of leafy green vegetables that nourish and strengthen us? What if we don't have to accept the traditional definition of the word 'grudge' – the one with negative connotations – but can instead create a better and more accurate definition that takes into account the full power of grudges? What if grudges can ward off danger? What if we could use them to help ourselves and others?

I've got some great news! It's not a case of 'What if?' All of these things are true. Holding grudges doesn't have to fill us with hate or make us bitter and miserable. If you approach the practice of grudge-holding in an enlightened way, you'll find it does the opposite: it makes you *more* forgiving. Your grudges can help you to honour your personal emotional landmarks, and you can distil vital life lessons from them – about your value system, your hopes, needs and priorities – that will act as a series of stepping stones, pointing you in the right direction for the best possible future.

Read on if you'd like to learn how to hold great grudges for a happier and more enlightened life . . . or even if you think my theory is probably wrong (I'll convince you by the end of this book – you see if I don't!) but you still quite fancy reading some entertaining and occasionally jaw-dropping true grudge stories.

The Grudge-holding Type

Some people admit, proudly and happily, to being the grudge-holding type. Others don't. When I announced on Twitter that I was writing this book, the reactions were varied and fascinating. Author Joanna Cannon said, 'I feed and water my grudges as if they were small, exotic plants, and I CANNOT WAIT to read this.' Another woman, Jules, said, 'Me and my sister specialise in "hold againsts". Our hold againsts are legion.'

I suspect that Joanna, Jules and I relate to our grudges in a similar way: we enjoy them and are proud of them and, since we feel that they have positive value for us, we see no reason to pretend we don't have them or to try to get rid of them. Personally, I don't believe it's possible to mix with other human beings on a regular basis and not collect some grudges – and it's not desirable either, unless you're one of those lucky people like Rachel, who responded online to the news of this book with the comment, 'I am a hopeless grudge-keeper. I struggle on for an hour at most. I think I'm basically too lazy. I hope this isn't a life-threatening condition.'

My son shares Rachel's laziness in relation to grudges. If someone is horrible to him, he just wants it to be over – not only because it's unpleasant but also, and mainly, because any kind of problem, anything that's made him angry or upset, is something he's fundamentally not interested in. All he wants is to stop thinking about it – not in a denial kind of way but in a 'who even cares? Just go away' way. Unpleasantness, the second it's over, rolls off him like rain-drops off the waxed bonnet of a car.

I'm different. I've always wanted any present-moment meanness or poor treatment of me (or anyone else) to stop so that I can *start* thinking about it – because what could be more gripping, right? Is the person who did me this particular wrong dangerous, or was it a one-off? What should I think about them from now on? How should I treat them? Every time, it's a mystery that needs to be solved, and I'm a mystery addict. (This probably explains why my day job is writing crime fiction and my hobby is reading it.)

My daughter is exactly like me. She gets very upset if someone is mean, spiteful, neglectful or unfair to her or anybody she cares about – far more upset than my son does – but she *is* interested in nastiness and all the bad things people do, because they're part of human behaviour, which is the main thing in life that fascinates her. She likes to analyse it, and to try to make it fit into a coherent overarching narrative. So do I. I think this explains why my daughter and I are dedicated and passionate grudge-holders, while my son can't be bothered and genuinely doesn't seem to have any grudges at all.

My son's way of not holding grudges is, I suspect, the only healthy and harmless way to hold no grudges. In grudge-holding terms, I see my son as a tree trunk with no concentric circles in it. Those grudge rings simply aren't there – that's just how that particular tree has grown, and that's fine.

What Would a Grudge Look Like?

During the researching and writing of this book, I thought a lot about what grudges might look like if they had a physical form. I started to picture grudges as if they were concrete things. A ring in the trunk of a tree was the first image that came to mind; then a cactus (lots of spikes), then a small square box wrapped in beautiful coloured paper with a bow around it. I asked people to send me their drawings and ideas about what grudges might look like. I was sent two pictures that I loved. One was a round red ball or sphere cupped in someone's hands. Words and phrases were dangling from the fingers of the hands: things like 'broken hearts', 'forgotten birthdays' and 'unfair dismissal'. The other was a kind of cloud-shaped grumpy grudge creature. (You can see both on the 'How to Hold a Grudge' page of my website!)

I suspect that the person who drew the grumpy-little-creature grudge would feel and think differently about grudges than me, given that the image I finally fixed on was a gift-wrapped box. I didn't ask my son to draw me a picture, but if I had, I'm sure he'd have rolled his eyes and said, 'Nah. CBA.' That stands for 'Can't be arsed.' Of course he can't – he is fundamentally not interested in grudges.

That's absolutely fine. I'm not even going to cut him out of my will or accuse him of being no son of mine or anything like that. And it's fine for my son – and anyone like him in this respect, anyone whose mind spontaneously and effortlessly ejects all bad things the moment they're over because they find them as dull as I find anecdotes about the history of the steam engine (my fault – I'm not blaming steam engines) – to hold no grudges at all.

But what if, like most people, you have a mind that still remembers every detail of the time your supposedly best friend told your deepest secret to the postman without permission? What if you find yourself secretly thinking 'Fuck you' every time your cousin comes to visit, because she once fed chocolate to your dog and made him ill? If you're that sort of person – and I believe most of us are – then trying not to hold grudges when all your instincts are screaming, 'No, really, I'm pretty sure this is grudgeworthy' is a very bad idea.

'That sort of person'? What sort do I mean?

Why, an ordinary person, of course. A perfectly regular person of the everyday kind. Regular, ordinary people get upset when people upset us. We feel betrayed when those we trust betray us. We get angry when we're wronged, slandered, poked in the eye with a sharp stick or unreasonably imposed upon. Denial or repression of our natural grudge-holding instinct is bad for us and it's bad for the world. (Chapter 6 of this book explains why, but please don't skip ahead – that's an author–reader grudge waiting to happen right there. You need to read the book in the right order, or the arguments won't make sense.)

Trainer, mentor and therapist Anne Grey agrees that trying to suppress our emotions is not advisable. She said: 'It's a natural response to feel emotions like hurt, sadness, anger. Allow the intense emotion to be there without judging it.'

Many of us have been trained from a young age to think that holding grudges is a petty, compassionless and horrible thing to do. This means that as we go through life and every so often find ourselves on the receiving end of treatment that's somewhere on the shoddy-to-heinous spectrum, we are ill-equipped to deal with it in the best and wisest way. One of the responses to my announcement of this book was: 'Ooh! How does this grudge-holding work?! I think of them as mean, grim obstacles to moving on and letting go!' I loved this response, because it neatly set out for me the challenge I faced: convincing people who've been trained to think that holding grudges is a negative and harmful thing to do that a) it's not, it's the opposite, because b) they've been thinking about grudges, and using the word, in the wrong way all these years. The purpose of this book is to give you a more psychologically accurate definition to work with – one that will make you a) think about grudges in a different and more optimistic way for ever and b) want to start collecting your own.

Once I had committed to writing this book, I asked people

to send me their grudges if they wanted to. So many people I asked looked mildly alarmed and said, 'I'm not sure I have any. I don't think I hold grudges.'

'Oh, okay, that's fine,' I said. 'So let me ask you a different question: is there anyone who you feel differently about now, because of something they once did?' At that point, almost everyone perked up and said, 'Oh, yes! My mother wore white to my wedding', or 'My stepmom bought the coat I wanted . . . and then never wore it', or 'A girl from the B team deliberately tripped me up and injured me so that she could get my place on the A team.'

Over and over again, people told me they didn't hold grudges and couldn't think of any at all, then went on to offer something that they claimed wasn't a grudge but that, according to my definition, was *exactly what a grudge should be.*

We're going to look in more detail about what grudges are, aren't and should be in Chapters 2 and 3. For now, all I will say is: if you think of grudges as 'mean, grim obstacles to moving on', then when someone asks you if you have any, you're obviously not going to leap up enthusiastically, hand in the air, and say, 'Yes! Yes, I do! Let me give you a full, walkaround tour of my grudge collection!' Who wants to think of themselves as mean or grim? I'm going to show you that grudges are protective, life-enhancing and fun. I hope that once you've read this book, you will understand that sending yourself and your loved ones out into the world with a strong grudge-growing ability is as essential as putting on a helmet and not drinking four bottles of vodka before getting onto your motorbike and zooming off down the motorway. Trust me: it's true.

And now I want to ask you a question: if someone were

to ask you to name your top five grudges, could you? I could, though I'd probably come back ten minutes later to announce that I'd already revised the order, and numbers three and four had swapped places in my chart. I might also try to start a discussion (because, yes, I *am* that kind of weird person) about what 'top' means, in this context. Most serious? Most enjoyable to hold?

Wait – enjoyable? Some of you will be wondering, 'How could holding a grudge ever be enjoyable? How could it be anything but bitter, hateful and corrosive?' If that's what you're thinking, then you've come to the right place. You are the very person I had in mind when I first became aware of a burning urge to write this book, because you're the person I need to convince that, handled correctly, grudges can be good for you – and not only good, but great. If, on the other hand, you're grinning and saying to yourself, 'Of *course* grudges can be fun – who could doubt it?' then you are my kindred spirit and I've written this book for you too (and you, especially, will love it. Unless you enjoy your grudges for the wrong reasons, which we'll come to in due course).

Let me start with a grudge story that will always have a special place in my heart, for a very particular reason . . .

Michael Upside Down in the Doorway

A few years ago, I went to Exeter in South-West England for a work-related event. It was an evening event, and there was no possibility of me getting home the same night. Luckily, I had close friends who lived a short drive from Exeter –

friends I'd known for many years. They had a spare room and were only too happy to put me up for the night. My friends were a married couple with children and a dog, but both children had left home some years earlier, and only the husband, the wife and the dog are relevant to this story. I'm going to call them Michael, Linda and Hobart respectively. Hobart was a small Border terrier who liked to nestle in warm places: his bed, other people's beds, amid piles of woolly jumpers in drawers and wardrobes.

The whole family loved Hobart, but Michael was obsessive about him. In order to relax he needed to know, at all times, where in the house Hobart was. Even if he had no reason to fear for the dog's safety or well-being, it wasn't enough for Michael to know that Hobart was somewhere or other nearby; he had to know Hobart's exact location. If he went out, the first question he would ask Linda on his return was 'Where's Hobart?', and if she couldn't give him a precise answer ('on the blue chair in the kitchen' or 'sitting next to the radiator in the lounge') he would express disapproval, as if she had been negligent in her Hobart-monitoring duties.

I was well aware that if I spent a night at Michael's house, there was a strong chance I would witness some Hobart-related peculiarity. On previous visits I had been asked a) if I'd be willing to give up my armchair and sit on a hard chair instead, because Michael suspected Hobart might want to sit where I was sitting, and b) if I wouldn't mind sleeping with my door open, in case Hobart wanted to wander in and out of the guest room during the night. As charmingly as I could, and hoping I wouldn't cause offence, I refused on both occasions, and Michael accepted my refusals with good grace.

I had never minded any of this. I found it amusing. Michael

was the first to laugh at himself and admit that he was neurotic about his dog, so I was happy to spend time at the house. I also found it fascinating that Linda, who did not share Michael's neurosis, was willing to pander to it so comprehensively, monitoring Hobart's movements on a second-by-second basis, so that if ever Michael were to appear and ask 'Where's Hobart?', she would have an answer ready.

On this particular night, I arrived at Michael and Linda's house at around ten o'clock, and we all had a cup of tea together. At eleven, I said that I was going to bed. Eleven is early by my normal standards, but at the time I had two children under three years old, both of whom woke up often in the night, and I was also frantically busy writing a book while holding down a part-time job that was an hour and a half's drive from where I lived, and travelling at least once a week to a poetry reading or event.

I explained to Michael and Linda that I was exhausted, that I had to get up early to drive home the next day and that I wanted to make the most of this night that would be blissfully free of interruptions from babies and toddlers. Then I went to bed and sank into a deep sleep.

The next thing I knew, I was jolting awake, clutching the duvet to my body like a shield. The adrenaline coursing through my body told me something was wrong. Sleep-befuddled and shocked, I found it hard to work out what had happened, but there were three significant clues: the light in my room was on, the door to the landing was wide open and Michael appeared to be suspended upside down in the doorway. His head was lower than his body, and close to the floor.

It took me only a few seconds to realise that he was not,

in fact, hanging upside down from the door frame. His head was near the floor, though; I'd been right about that. He was bent double, with his head next to his feet, looking under the bed – the same bed that contained his freaked-out house guest.

I remember feeling like an idiot, and wanting to cry because I'd been stupid enough to trust that I had a night of unbroken sleep ahead of me. At home, I could handle being woken up. I expected it; I slept in a new-mother-on-call kind of way. This was worse than being woken by my children, which I at least understood and didn't react to with panic. In those first few seconds, I could think of no non-alarming reason for Michael to have opened the door to the room where I was sleeping, turned on the light and bent himself in half.

I waited for him to say sorry for disturbing me – for coming into the room where I was sleeping and *actually turning the light on*. He didn't apologise. Nor did he seem to notice my shocked gasp and duvet-clutching. 'I thought Hobart might be in here with you,' he said. 'I can't find him.'

He came closer, knelt down and stuck his head right under the bed. When he emerged, he said with a sigh, 'No, he's not under there.' He then opened, one by one, every cupboard door and drawer in the room.

I can't remember what I was wearing. I am the opposite of a nocturnally glamorous person, so it's likely to have been an old, frayed T-shirt. It wasn't anything too revealing, which I was relieved about – though of course if Hobart had gone missing, that was more important than Michael possibly seeing me without many clothes on.

As I was thinking this, I heard Linda call out, 'Found him, Michael! He's in here, on the sofa.' 'Here' turned out to be Michael's study.

As I heard these words, I had the strangest feeling: as if something had opened up in my mind, or broken in, and rearranged all my thoughts. 'This is a significant moment,' I said to myself silently, even though I hadn't yet fully worked out why.

Without a word to me, Michael set off to verify Linda's claim, turning off the light in the guest room and closing the door on his way out. His study was the room next to the guest room, where I was – separated from it only by a thin partition wall. This, too, struck me as important.

Once he was gone, I picked up my phone to check the time. Only half past midnight. I was determined to extract as much sleep from the rest of the night as I could, so I said to myself, 'Now isn't the time to work out what this means, but I *am* going to try and work it out soon, because it's important. I mustn't forget that it happened.' Having made that resolution, I soon fell asleep again and, thankfully, there were no more surprises for the rest of the night.

Anne Grey says: 'Working out what something means is a helpful way of responding. Another approach is to allow yourself to feel the natural emotion without judgement, and identify how you want to feel now. Being fully present now allows for greater clarity and wisdom to emerge, from your natural intuition or inner knowing.'

The next day, I thought about Michael being upside down in the doorway as I drove back to West Yorkshire, where I lived at the time, and I've thought about it many times since. It's a grudge I hold that involves Michael, but I wouldn't say I hold it *against* him, because it didn't stop me from liking him, and it didn't end our friendship. (As I'll explain in Chapter 2, we should hold grudges *about* people, not *against* them. A grudge shouldn't have any 'against' in it.)

While I didn't enjoy being woken in the night, I pitied Michael more than I blamed him. He was plainly not capable of rational behaviour where Hobart was concerned. I'd known this for years, even though that night was when I saw its most extreme expression. In a moment of neurosis, he'd felt compelled to burst into the room where I was sleeping. I don't think he meant me any harm – in fact, I know he didn't. Opening the door without knocking might well have been his attempt to avoid disturbing me. Perhaps he thought that if he didn't knock but just walked in, and then tiptoed around, I might not wake up (despite his having turned on the light).

Still, I hold a grudge about this incident, and it's one I want to keep. And this is a special grudge – one that deserves pride of place in my 'Grudge Cabinet' (to which I will introduce you later). Why, when Michael's behaviour was neither malicious nor especially damaging to me, am I determined to remember this episode? It's partly because it's the first grudge I was aware of *as a grudge* at the very moment it came into being. Previously, my grudge-holding followed a different pattern: something would happen, and I would realise afterwards that I was angry or upset about it. Then some time later I would find that, yes, it was still there and showed no sign of shifting.

With this incident – which I still think of as *Michael Upside Down in the Doorway*; I give all my grudges titles because it helps with cataloguing and classification – I was aware while it was happening that here was a grudge forming in real time, one that would stay with me for ever. Also, I noticed that, once I'd recovered from my initial shock at being woken so unexpectedly, I was neither angry nor upset. Instead, I was curious – certain that an important event had occurred, and eager to know what it meant.

It was a strange feeling, and also a turning point. Previously, I had formed all my grudges spontaneously and unintentionally. This was the first one that I consciously resolved to create because I sensed, in the moment, that some kind of inner exclamation mark or mental bookmark was required – in other words, a grudge, according to my definition of the word (though that wasn't how I put it to myself at the time, and it was only later that I fully came to understand what my definition was). On the night in question, all I knew was that this was a story that I needed first to polish, so that it was in its best possible form, and then to remember, and then to tell. The strangest thing of all was that I knew the main person to whom I needed to tell this story was myself.

That was thirteen years ago. Since then, I've got into the habit of doing this (let's call it 'mindful grudge creation'), and it's rare that I *don't* recognise a grudge-sparking incident as it's happening – but *Michael Upside Down in the Doorway* was my first. I didn't understand then why I needed to get the story right (and by right, I mean as clear and accurate as possible) or that it was a newly formed grudge. If you'd asked me then whether I held grudges, I probably wouldn't have admitted it, because I hadn't yet realised that grudges are really, *really* good for you.

Let's go back to Michael for a moment. When I thought about the *Upside Down in the Doorway* incident, several important features stood out:

1. Michael hadn't looked for Hobart in the rest of the house before interrupting my sleep. If he had, there would have been no story and no grudge. Michael's study, where Linda found Hobart, was next to the room I was in, and no one was sleeping in it. Why hadn't Michael checked there first? Why hadn't he checked the whole house before walking in on me? Why didn't my need for sleep and my privacy matter at least that much to him?

2. Waking me wasn't the only thing he risked doing by coming into the guest room unannounced. He also risked scaring me (which he did), and embarrassing me. For all he knew, I might have been sleeping in the nude.

3. He didn't, at any point, apologise. When someone wakes you up unnecessarily in the middle of the night, gets down on his knees by your bedside and then *doesn't apologise*, it's hard not to notice the missed opportunity. The next morning before I left, Michael didn't say, 'By the way, sorry about intruding on your sleep last night.' No light, cheery 'Soz about that!' was forthcoming. And I knew that wasn't because Michael was pleased that he'd made my night a bit worse than it needed to be. He simply hadn't thought then, and wasn't thinking now, about my needs or feelings. In his eyes, if I wasn't bleeding from the eyeballs or dangling out of a fifteenth-floor window, I was obviously fine . . . and that left him free to think only about his own needs.

I knew that Michael wasn't going to worry even for a second about having been a bad host, or that I might not be keen to stay *chez* him in future. I also knew that he would have jumped in front of a bullet to protect me if he perceived me to be in true danger. In many ways, he is a noble and self-sacrificing person. If I had been subject to a form of harm *that he recognised as harm*, he would have put my welfare before his own, I had no doubt – he'd have done so for me or for anyone he cared about. The trouble was (and this was one of the things that struck me as I drove back to Yorkshire, and I couldn't believe it had taken me so long to figure it out) Michael had a worrying tendency to define other people as being perfectly all right and not suffering any sort of adverse effects whenever it suited him to do so.

I realised that he was someone who would always be willing to cause me minor inconvenience, fleeting annoyance, mild alarm and low-key unhappiness if he needed to do so in order to alleviate his own anxiety or to get something he very much wanted, without stopping to question whether it was correct or fair. I understood clearly, after being only subliminally and vaguely aware of it for so many years, that I would always matter far less to Michael than he mattered to himself in any day-to-day life/non-crisis situation; he would always sacrifice my welfare for the sake of his own when it suited him to do so, as long as I seemed 'basically fine' to him. And he would always find a way to justify his behaviour, if challenged, and to make me feel terrible, because he was absolutely certain that he was a Very Good Person.

Therapist Anne Grey says: 'This behaviour in Michael is what could be described as "unconscious" behaviour, in that he is so absorbed in, and identified with, his thoughts and emotions that he is unaware of the impact on others and, more importantly, he is unaware that he has the choice to step back, observe, gain greater clarity and see that, if he wishes, there may be a different course of action available to him.'

The Grudge-fold Path

That feeling of significance I'd had in the middle of the night had been my subconscious saying, 'It's time you realised how this man will always behave.' Other stories sprang out from the recesses of my memory to join this newly minted one. Some related specifically to nights I had spent at Michael's house in the past. When I first knew him, his favourite thing to do in the morning was play loud music. If I was staying with him and still asleep, tough: I would be woken by loud Queen or Led Zeppelin songs. I didn't notice or mind particularly in those days, because I didn't yet have work I cared about, or children, and so excessive tiredness wasn't an issue for me. But thinking about it after the *Upside Down in the Doorway* incident, I remembered that whenever I asked Michael if he could wait to play his music until I was awake, he made it clear that this put him out quite a bit, and had a tiny tantrum about it.

On one occasion, instead of just going in a huff, he set out his case for me, like a defendant representing himself in court. 'Look,' he said. 'First thing in the morning, while I'm getting dressed and ready to go to work, that's my favourite time in the day. And listening to music – at a decent volume, so that I can *actually hear* it, is one of my favourite things to do. Why should I have to deprive myself of that just because you happen to be in my house?' When I asked him how he would feel if I were to play the *Oklahoma!* soundtrack really loudly while he was trying to sleep in my guest room, he looked confused and said, 'Well . . . obviously I'd hate it.'

'Well, then!' I said.

'Hmph,' he said, and remained grumpy for the next hour. Neither of us mentioned the fact that I had never done and would never do this, whereas he regularly did.

Michael only stopped playing very loud music first thing in the morning after I'd asked him to (and after he'd had a small, grown-up version of a tantrum) about four times.

On the journey home, the day after *Upside Down in the Doorway*, I thought of at least ten or twelve Significant Michael Stories. These were the first stories that I officially and proudly installed in my Grudge Cabinet!

INTRODUCING THE GRUDGE CABINET

Let me guess – you don't have one yet, and you had no idea you needed one? Well, you do. You'll soon understand why. A Grudge Cabinet is the only physical object you will need in order to practise enlightened grudge-holding of the sort I advocate, and the good news is: it doesn't have to be an actual cabinet whittled from the finest oak. It can be a shoe-box, an old handbag, a jewellery box, a bedside cabinet drawer . . . Any container will do. You will be using this container to store all the grudges you want to keep in order to enhance your life. If, like me, you're the proud owner of lots of great grudges, you'll need a larger box/bag/drawer.

Your Grudge Cabinet should take whatever form feels right and most appealing to you. If you love the idea of whittling an actual cabinet out of wood, please do so. If you want to buy a brand new designer handbag to be your Grudge Cabinet, great! Or, if you'd feel happier using a modest cardboard shoe box, that's wonderful – whatever works for you. (I'm sure you're wondering, so I'll tell you: I am still in the process of figuring out what I would like my Grudge Cabinet to be. I'm tempted by the designer handbag idea, but the words 'secret drawer' are also calling to me. For the time being, my Grudge Cabinet is this book and a file on my computer called 'Grudge Book Notes'.)

INTRODUCING THE GRUDGE-FOLD PATH

Practitioners of Buddhism follow the 'Eightfold Path' to enlightenment. I know enough about what this means to know that it's a path I could never personally follow. I follow, instead, The Grudge-fold Path (which I explain in detail in Chapter 7), and, once you've read this book, I hope some of you will too. If you have only eight grudges, then your Grudge-fold Path might happen to be eightfold as well, but I have named my Path so that it doesn't specify a number. It is versatile, therefore, and can work for you even if you have 347 grudges.

The 'fold' part of The Grudge-fold Path's name does not refer to the number of grudges that go towards making up the path. It refers, instead, to the physical act of folding. In

Chapter 8, I will tell you all about why and how to write up your grudge stories, and you will see that the folding is an important part of the grudge-curation ritual for Grudge-fold Path followers.

The *Upside Down in the Doorway* night wasn't the last night I spent under the same roof as Michael. There were several occasions afterwards when avoiding it would have been too difficult, but I never again willingly and freely chose it, and I felt protected and less likely to suffer once I had my grudge fixed securely in place: a story that gave me official permission to link it to other Michael stories and say to myself: 'Remember: Michael is this sort of person, likely to behave in this way.'

I learned from *Michael Upside Down in the Doorway* – and the other Michael stories that flocked to join it – that, while continuing to pursue the friendship and be nice to him, and while not resenting him or feeling anger towards him, I should be aware and on my guard in his presence, and not let him do me any harm, *according to my definition of harm,* which I gave myself permission to believe was every bit as important as his.

The forming of the grudge – identifying and clarifying the story, and interpreting what it meant – gave me something practical to do in the moment that the annoying incident was taking place, so that I didn't feel angry or upset. I was too busy doing something far more constructive. It felt like being an observer of one's own life, thinking 'So what's the story here? Does it remind me of any other linked stories, containing the same main characters? And how should she respond? What's she thinking now?' She, of course, was me.

The *Michael Upside Down in the Doorway* story still feels very relevant; there is still a live charge associated with it in my mind. I see this charge as a helpful little bell that rings in my memory (there's another visual image of what a grudge might look like) reminding me that I might need to protect myself from Michael in future.

How might this little bell benefit me? Psychotherapist Helen Acton says: 'It's a familiar trope within psychoanalytic thinking that "those who cannot remember the past are condemned to repeat it", as most famously stated by philosopher George Santayana. It is Sophie's determination to remember and preserve her grudge-sparking incidents that offers her protection from the risk of finding herself in a similarly painful position again. Such vigilance ensures she is condemned to repeat nothing. Or at least she's offering herself the best chance in an uncertain and unpredictable world.'

I value and love my *Michael Upside Down in the Doorway* grudge, as I do all the grudges I deem worthy of keeping in and adding to my Grudge Cabinet. I'm grateful for my grudges because they have taught me, more than anything else in my life, the way I do and don't want to live.

Helen Acton agrees: 'For me, Sophie has here put her finger on the most valuable aspect of the Grudge-fold Path. It is a means by which to clarify her own personal value system. We all have one, but surprisingly few of us are able to understand or articulate what it might be until a line is crossed – a line that allows us to define a value by which we wish to live and by which we expect others to live. Having an understanding of our personal value system offers a basis on which to make decisions for ourselves, and a valuable tool with which to shape our lives. A well-held grudge is a statement of our own moral code. Added to that, it increases the likelihood that we will treat ourselves with self-respect, and therefore expect and demand to be treated respectfully by others. It is a way of saying to oneself, as Winston Churchill so pithily put it, "This is the sort of bloody nonsense up with which I will not put".'

The Importance of Stories

Over the years, I have read and loved hundreds of self-help books of the Buddhism-influenced variety, and also of the Christianity-influenced kind. The first that springs to mind is *The Power of Now* by Eckhart Tolle, which maintains that it's the stories we tell ourselves about our life experiences that upset us. We could easily, Tolle argues, tell ourselves a different story. This is totally true . . . if you can do it. Let's look at an example:

It's your fiftieth birthday. As a birthday treat, your wife is taking you out for dinner at your favourite restaurant, which has to be booked months in advance. You agree to meet her there at 7.30 p.m. You've been looking forward to it for weeks. She doesn't arrive. You sit there for several hours, then give up and go home. You find your wife in the living room. As you walk in, she says, 'Sorry I didn't turn up. I just didn't feel like going out this evening. I'm knackered.' You ask why she didn't ring or text to let you know, and she says, 'Huh? Oh, sorry. I've been caught up in this TV series I'm hooked on.'

Based on my many careful readings of Eckhart Tolle, I'm certain he would advocate telling that story to oneself in the following way, in order to avoid unnecessary unhappiness: 'A man goes to a restaurant, sits there for a while, then returns home. A woman stays at home and doesn't go to the restaurant.' If you frame it in that way, Tolle claims, then you avoid all the suffering you would inflict upon yourself if you instead told the story as follows: 'She *knows* I've been looking forward to this for weeks, the selfish cow! And it's my *fiftieth*! A landmark birthday! She obviously doesn't give a shit about me.'

Tolle believes we can eliminate all suffering from our lives simply by *not* telling ourselves upsetting stories in which people have behaved like dicks and hurt our feelings. Other self-help books I've read – the majority – would concede that, if you wanted to tell a true version of that story, you would need to acknowledge that some pretty selfish behaviour was involved. *But* (those same books would argue) we shouldn't allow other people's inconsiderateness or even their cruelty to make us unhappy and affect our inner peace. We should simply tell ourselves that their bad behaviour is their problem, not ours.

Brooke Castillo, whose weekly podcast 'The Life Coach School' I find completely addictive, teaches something called 'The Model', in which Circumstances (the wife not showing up at the restaurant for the planned birthday dinner) are seen as inherently neutral, connected to Feelings and only able to cause Feelings (hurt, unhappiness/bitterness) via Thoughts ('How could she do that to me? The selfish bitch!').

Castillo argues that no one can hurt our feelings or make us suffer unless we let them. No one, she claims, can make us feel any way at all, positive or negative, because we are in charge of our own feelings, and we always have the power to change those feelings by changing our thoughts about particular circumstances. This approach is similar to Tolle's (he says 'story we tell ourselves', she says 'thought', but effectively they mean the same thing). Castillo acknowledges Tolle as one of her main teachers and influences.

On one level, they're both absolutely right: if you can change your thoughts, or tell yourself completely different stories, then, yes, of course you can change the way you feel. The problem for most of us is that when we try to think the new, hurt-avoiding thought – 'It's great that my sister shagged my husband! I'm so thrilled about it!' – we might not succeed entirely in convincing ourselves.

I was once told by a boyfriend's mother that if my life was in danger, she probably wouldn't try to save me. Not definitely; only probably. Then she shook her head, pondering it anew and concluded, 'No, I just don't think I would.' She said all this completely out of the blue – just in case any of you are imagining I prompted it by saying, 'Hey, bitch, bet you wouldn't lift a finger to rescue me from a burning building, would you?'

Now, I could tell myself that story as Tolle would advise me to: 'A woman made a comment to another woman, and there's no way of knowing what she intended when she said it.' I could think a thought that would avoid hurt, as Castillo might suggest: 'My boyfriend's mum can't make me suffer because her words and thoughts are her problem and responsibility, and I know my life is valuable no matter what she says.'

However – and it's quite a large however, not a little one – I'd be willing to bet everything I own that *it will always be true for the vast majority of humans that, when people say hurtful things and do appalling things to them, they will be hurt and appalled as a result.* In that context, the more neutral, less painful story you're trying to tell yourself might not 'take' because, not to put too fine a point on it, it feels to you like a whopping great lie. And if you're not convinced by it, you won't feel better. You risk feeling much worse, in fact, if you start to think of your attempt to lie to yourself as yet another shitty thing you've suffered.

Helen Acton says: 'Here we find the crucial distinction between the 'ideals' of the positive psychology movement and people's *actual lived experience.* It is only by attending to her actual lived experience of the feelings an experience has caused – feelings of betrayal, offence, wounding of any kind – that Sophie will find a way to move past it and it has any chance of losing its painful emotional charge. To simply slap a smiley sticker over the truth of the experience is to deny the truth of the human condition, which is that we are social animals, we live in a relational world and we are impacted and affected in every moment by others. As Sophie says, the smiley sticker feels like a lie, because it is a lie. The existential philosophers would say it is a way of living in "bad faith".'

In her podcast, Brooke Castillo admits that she has to do regular 'thought work', as she calls it, in order not to suffer the hurt and anger that would otherwise result from events like someone trying to defraud her, which is one of the examples she gives.

I too have tried to do endless thought work over the years. At a certain point, I realised that, though I knew all the theory off by heart – I'd have got 100 per cent in any Enlightened Guru Miscellanea exam – I nevertheless couldn't put into practice what any of my favourite gurus were advising. I'd tried to think only positive thoughts all the time, and to tell myself that my inner peace would henceforth be unaffected by the dreadful or callous behaviour of other people, but I knew, deep down, that it was an act, and quite impossible from a practical point of view.

For about two years, I was able to fake it and appear marginally enlightened (though maybe I'm kidding myself here. My sister frequently said to me, 'You're not *really* enlightened, are you? You still want to bitch about people, don't you? And goddamnit, she was right! I did). As I pretended to be all-forgiving, my grudge stories got louder in my head.

Then one day – around three months before *Michael Upside Down in the Doorway* – I had a breakthrough: it wasn't that I *couldn't* give up my grudges. It was that I didn't want to – because they were wondrous things.

Anne Grey says: 'At no stage do we need to judge ourselves for having these thoughts or emotions, or pretend they're not there. We're simply allowing what is, and then crucially, in this moment now, seeing we have a choice.'

I realised that my grudges were the very route to positivity and well-being that I was after! They weren't harming me or anyone else. I had no negative feelings associated with them at all; they were simply a collection of stories that were important to me, and that I wanted to keep. More than that: I suddenly saw how our grudges could be not just good for us, but great. And if that was true, then what the hell were all these gurus doing encouraging us to give up our gorgeous grudges? Do they *want* us unarmed when the toughest things happen to us? If so, why?

I had always enjoyed telling other people about my grudges; now I wondered why. If grudges are so bad for us, where was this contentment kick coming from? The whole subject of grudges, I realised, was desperately under-examined and much misunderstood.

As I researched the topic, I learned that I was not, as I'd previously suspected, too bitchy for enlightenment. A contradiction that I'd been aware of in myself suddenly no longer needed explaining, because it wasn't a contradiction. There is no one – not one single person on earth – to whom I wouldn't give a second chance. I also have more grudges than anyone I know, and a greater interest in and appetite for them. *These two statements do not contradict each other.* They fit together perfectly once you understand that holding grudges is the ideal route to being a more forgiving and happier person.

To go back for a moment to the wife who didn't show up for the fiftieth birthday dinner . . . In that scenario, or a similar one, thinking only neutral and positive thoughts in the hope of avoiding suffering is *not* the answer. We can't avoid suffering, so let's not waste time trying. Hating and feeling bitter and full of rage is *also* not the answer. Constructing a grudge, holding it (in a safe, responsible and uplifting way) and *then* forgiving the person – which is *much* easier once you've got a solid grudge in place – is the answer.

This book will explain exactly and in detail how that's possible, and why it's the way forward.

The Grudge Quiz

'Forgive your enemies – nothing annoys them more.'

Oscar Wilde

Before we get going on the theory, here's a quiz. Let's find out what kind of grudge-holder you are! These questions are aimed at illuminating your present attitude and approach to grudges. At the end of the book there will be another quiz, to see if your views about grudges have altered at all.

1. You notice that your best friend has liked several 'I have great news!' posts on social media by someone you loathe. Your friend has always claimed to dislike this person too, and to be totally on your side – yet here they are, favouriting posts that celebrate your enemy. Do you:

a) End the friendship and cut your friend out of your life.

b) Ask your friend why they have done this, and if they have lied to you about sharing your dislike of this person.

c) Assume they must still be on your side despite this new evidence, and tell yourself they must have hit the like button by mistake, or done it in an ironic, not-really-liking way?

d) Continue with the friendship, say nothing and hold a secret grudge.

2. You have always praised your friend Bob enthusiastically whenever he has done something impressive. Then you achieve something amazing and Bob doesn't give you anywhere near the same amount of praise. He says, 'I can see you put a lot of effort into it,' without saying whether he thinks the effort was worth it or if he enjoyed or hated the end product. You realise that he has never praised you properly, or enthused about any of your achievements – it's just something he never does. Do you:

a) Decide never to praise him again.

b) Tell him that his reaction hurt you, and explain why.

c) Praise him even more than you would normally, in order to lead by example, hoping he takes the hint.

d) Pity him – how awful not to be able to express enthusiasm! – amend your opinion of him in the downward direction and tell yourself he hasn't got away with anything because you will never feel the same way about him again?

3. Which of these pairs of quotes appeals to you the most?

a) 'I don't hold grudges. We good. You may not hear from me ever again, but we good.' (anonymous/many internet sources)/'I have a limit, and when you reach it I dismiss you from my life. It's that simple.' (anonymous/many internet sources)

b) 'At the heart of all anger, all grudges, and all resentment, you'll always find a fear that hopes to stay anonymous.' Donald L. Hicks, *Look Into the Stillness*/'Before I took a stand, I was always . . . confused about my rights and about what was real' – psychotherapist Sandy Katz

c) 'I forgive people, but that doesn't mean I accept their behaviour or trust them. I forgive them for me, so I can let go and move on with my life.' (anonymous/many internet sources)/'I don't hold grudges. I remember facts.' (anonymous/many internet sources)

d) 'They say it's good to let your grudges go, but I don't know, I'm quite fond of my grudge. I tend it like a little pet.' From *Big Little Lies* by Liane Moriarty/'Can I petition to make holding grudges an Olympic event? Cause I've been in training my whole life.' Anna Kendrick on Twitter

4. You tell your friend Beatrice that her sister Jane (also your friend) has scratched your car and lied about it to avoid paying for repairs. Beatrice reacts aggressively and says, 'It's a crap, hideous car anyway.' Do you:

a) Think of both Beatrice and Jane as 'dead to you', and banish them from your life.

b) Understand that Beatrice must have been horrified to hear that her own sister was a lying car-scratcher, and so probably lashed out at you without meaning to. Once she calms down, you'll talk to her again and give her the chance to react more appropriately.

c) Decide that Beatrice was only mean to you because she was so upset herself, and almost certainly regretted dissing your car a second after she had done so. You forgive her instantly, no questions asked – you know she didn't mean to be cruel.

d) Make a mental note that neither Beatrice nor Jane cares about justice or your feelings – so from now on you won't care quite so much about their feelings or any unfair treatment they receive, though you might continue with the friendship and enjoy their company sometimes because if you were to ditch or boycott them, it might cause problems among your wider circle of friends?

5. You try to reserve a table at a restaurant, Fred's, for 7 p.m. Fred, the owner, tells you that this is impossible because they have two sittings, 6 until 8 and 8 until late. You explain that you want a table at 7, not 6 or 8, and that 7 is a reasonable time to want to have dinner. Fred won't budge. Do you:

a) Tell him you think he's unreasonable to put profit before customers' wishes and needs, resolve never to go to his restaurant again and tell everyone you meet what happened in the hope of putting others off going there too.

b) Suggest that perhaps Fred should reconsider his policy because it's not ideal for customers, and then book a table for 6 or 8 p.m. instead, or go somewhere else.

c) Decide that, actually, there are advantages to going at 6 – you'd have time to see a movie afterwards. Or see the early show and eat at 8. All's well that ends well!

d) Don't argue or protest, but resolve to boycott Fred's restaurant in future because of the unreasonable policy.

RESULTS

Mostly 'a's – you are **The Cut-Off Queen (or King)**

THE GOOD NEWS: You know how to protect yourself. You are therefore likely to be treated better and taken advantage of much less often than more tolerant, lenient people. You recognise your own worth and rightly expect good, kind, reasonable behaviour from those around you. You trust your judgement as much as anybody else's, and you're clever enough not to waste time and energy on those who don't deserve it.

THE BAD NEWS: You might be a little too defensive. There may be times when a more nuanced approach is called for. Be careful that your willingness to cut people off doesn't lead to you losing people you would benefit from keeping in your life. Don't become too cut-off happy, and take care that you don't start to feel proud of cutting people off. Also, check you're not, deep down, motivated by fear (of the continuing relationship, and what it might require of you emotionally or psychologically, for example facing up to the fact that there might be another side to the story as valid as your own). Often we make decisions based on fear and disguise it as a principled stance. Strange but true fact: the more you are motivated by fear, the more others will be afraid of you, and you don't (or shouldn't) want that.

Mostly 'b's – you are **The Empathetic Analyst**

THE GOOD NEWS: you are analytical, and keen to give everybody a fair chance. You're interested in learning the psychological motivation for a person's behaviour and, until you understand, you don't condemn. This means that when you do hold grudges or cut someone out of your life, it's likely to be after careful consideration of mitigating circumstances and nuances, and some form of cost–benefit analysis. This is a responsible, mature approach.

THE BAD NEWS: not everyone is acting in similarly good faith. You might be too tolerant and open to those who will harm you. Be especially careful of repeat offenders.

Mostly 'c's – you are **The Easy-Lifer**

THE GOOD NEWS: you hate causing trouble, for yourself or for others. This is great! You have peaceful instincts, which is a brilliant quality to have. Wherever possible, you will find a way to plough on through life without making a fuss that anyone has to deal with, which means your life might well be stress-free and fun most of the time.

THE BAD NEWS: you can be naive, and spend long periods hibernating in a state of denial. The danger here is that, in spite of your conflict-avoiding instincts, someone close to you could bring trouble into your life, and you wouldn't recognise the danger and develop an appropriate defence. It might be worth facing facts and your feelings more squarely, and making sure you're not lying to yourself about anything.

Mostly 'd's – you are **The Grudge Guru**

You are a natural and expert grudge-holder! You can probably skip the next chapter, in which 'grudge' is defined, or just cross it out and write your own definition, which is bound to be at least as good as mine.

THE GOOD NEWS: you are capable of protecting yourself, while extracting maximum enjoyment from your grudges and seeing the funny side of them wherever possible. At the same time, you don't cut people off – so if someone's behaviour changes or improves, you can forgive or amend your opinion.

THE BAD NEWS: you often need to be 'two-faced' and pretend to be perfectly okay with people you secretly can't bear. This can be tiring, and you risk losing touch with your own inner truth. Also, you might start to relish grudge-holding a bit too much. Be careful that it doesn't become a hobby. You don't want to find yourself creating unnecessary grudges to feed your addiction. Only make a grudge out of something that deserves and needs to be one.

I am type 'd': the Grudge Guru. This should surprise nobody. Whichever type you are, you can use the Grudge-fold Path to make sure that you reap all the rewards available to all great grudge-holders, and avoid all the pitfalls.

2

What Grudges Are,
What They Aren't and
What They Should Be

Grudge n. a long-lasting feeling of resentment or dislike
(Oxford English Dictionary)

*a persistent feeling of resentment, esp one due to some cause,
such as an insult or injury*
(Collins English Dictionary)

*a grudge is a bad feeling or hate you hold against another person
for something bad they did, or you think they did, to you.*
(Urban Dictionary)

*bitterness, rancor, malevolence, enmity, hatred. Grudge, malice, spite
refer to ill will held against another or others. A grudge is a feeling
of resentment harbored because of some real or fancied wrong.*
(dictionary.com)

I disagree with the definitions above. Or rather, I accept that
they define what a grudge *can* be and often is, but I know

they don't describe what a grudge *has* to be, and I don't believe they accurately reflect what a grudge *ought* to be.

When we speak of grudges, we use words like *hold, harbour, bear*. 'Hold' suggests tenacity or clinging, 'harbour' implies something hunted and vulnerable to which we have offered refuge. 'Bear' has connotations of pregnancy and motherhood. Is a grudge an unfortunate affliction or a prized possession?

In middle English, the word *grutch* meant to grouse or complain. There are late-middle-English words like *grudgen* and *gruggen*, which in turn derive from the old French word *grouchier*. This will sound familiar to most modern readers: someone who complains and grumbles more than others might, even today, be described as 'grouchier'. This derivation is kind of unfortunate for my purposes but it's a historical fact, so there's not much I can do about it. Still, I'm hoping that by the time you reach the end of this book, you'll have learned how to talk about your grudges not in a grouchy way but in a tone of joyful celebration.

What's Wrong With the Traditional Definitions?

I hate to sound grouchy, but there's plenty wrong with them. Let's look at the two main problems:

1) A grudge is not always the result of a 'real or fancied wrong'. It's quite possible to hold a grudge knowing that your grudgee (get used to this term – I'll be using

it again) has done nothing wrong at all. Let's say your best friend since childhood starts to date and subsequently marries your brother. There is no moral reason whatsoever why she shouldn't do this, but you might still hold a grudge about it. Couldn't she have chosen a different bloke instead of putting you in this bind that you hate, where two different parts of your world have suddenly collided and you now have to worry that she will develop a greater loyalty to him than to you, and end up telling him all your secrets? Knowing that your best friend and brother have technically done nothing wrong might make your grudge against them even stronger: they've shaken your world to the core without blotting their copybooks at all from an ethical point of view. You have no reason to object to their actions, and everyone would point this out immediately if you slagged them off anywhere apart from in your own head. How infuriating! As a result, you might resent them all the more.

I could give many examples of this sort. Imagine your Aunt Doreen buys the house next door to yours when it comes up for sale. You're outraged that she's invaded your territory in this way without first asking you how you'd feel about it. At the same time, you recognise that she has as much right to buy that house as any stranger, and it's not up to you to dictate where she ought to live, or who ought to live in the house next to yours.

Sometimes, there is neither insult nor injury involved – not even 'fancied' insult or injury (in other words, the mistaken belief that you've been wronged when you haven't). You might hold a grudge against a person for doing something that is actively good, even something that benefits you. Let's say your colleague Philip regularly makes the office stink by heating up fish for lunch in the communal microwave. Your work-station is right next to the office kitchen, and one day you decide you can't bear the stench any longer. You take Philip to one side and say, 'Listen, Phil . . . surely you can see that this is not on?' You explain that the smell is unbearable. He ignores you, insists that he has every right to heat up fish for his lunch, and continues to do so. Then one day a new recruit joins the firm: Nadine. Philip falls madly in love with Nadine on the spot. A week later, Nadine has a word with Philip about the fish, explaining just as you did that it's making the whole office stink. Philip agrees, apologises, sees the error of his ways and never heats up fish lunches in the microwave again.

Now, this is obviously a great result for everyone in the office, including you – but you might hold a 'Right Thing, Too Late' grudge about it. (In Chapter 3, we will be categorising grudges by identifying their key themes.) Or you might hold a 'Right Thing, Wrong Reasons' grudge. You'd have to be a saint not to. And your grudge wouldn't be about the fish-heating (though that might be a separate grudge you choose to hold) – it would relate specifically to the *good* things Philip had done: the stopping, the apologising, the new better behaviour: 'He does the right thing *now*? For *her*? After telling me I was dead wrong all the times *I* told him his behaviour was unacceptable?' In that exact situation, I suspect you might think less of Philip than you would if he never decided to do the right thing, and instead carried on being a warmer of smelly fish. I know I would!

2) Resentment, dislike, bitterness, rancour, malevolence, enmity, hatred, malice, spite, ill will . . . Blimey! (Why am I suddenly talking like a Cockney chimney sweep? It must be because I'm in shock.) Look at all those negative words! The traditional definitions of 'grudge' tend to suggest that holding grudges necessarily involves having negative, unpleasant feelings towards someone – not only having them fleetingly, but also deciding to hang on to them. In fact, grudges needn't involve clinging on to *any negative feelings at all,* as I will explain later.

The question 'Is holding grudges a hateful and negative thing to do?' is crucial in determining how we respond when asked, 'Do you hold grudges?' If we see them as nasty, petty, shameful things to have in our hearts and lives, we're likely to deny that we have any. Thankfully, we can look at grudges differently; we can see them as valuable souvenirs from our past – the important artefacts of our emotional and psychological history.

Imagine a visitor comes to your town and you're showing her round. At the centre of the market square, there's an extremely tall, rectangular sculpture made of grey marble. On it are carved the names of twenty-five people, and the words 'We will never forget you. Rest in peace.'

'What's this?' asks the visitor. 'Whose names are

these? What does it mean?' You tell her they're the names of all the window cleaners who died when the now infamous managing director of a local firm opened his twenty-eighth-floor window one day, walked out onto the scaffolding and pushed all twenty-five men who were cleaning the windows at that moment to their deaths. (He did it because he was trying to have an important meeting and their soaping and scraping of the windows was distracting him, in case you're wondering.)

Imagine your visitor shakes her head in a regretful, knowing, more-enlightened-than-thou way and says, 'That sounds horrible, but y'know, you're only going to upset yourself by dwelling on it, all you local residents. You should tear this commemorative statue down, build a McDonald's here instead and just move on. McDonald's is really cool! Everyone would be happier!'

Think how shocked you'd be to hear those words, and that advice, in that context. Think of the horrified reactions that would follow if someone said that about any real monument that's been erected to honour the memory of people who have died tragically and unjustly. In a public, political or historical context, everyone understands that, when something awful happens, forgetting about it and moving on *as if it didn't happen* is not always the best or right course of action. That's why people tend lovingly to cemetery plots years after the death of a loved one; it's why we take flowers and teddy bears and leave them at the site of a fatal traffic accident. We can see, in such situations, that this behaviour makes perfect sense. If your loved one dies suddenly of an aneurysm, no one says, 'Hey, don't waste a day on a funeral – that's too negative. Move on! Treat yourself to a lovely spa day instead.' No one says it the day after the death, and no one would say it a decade later either, on the tenth anniversary. 'You're not *still* going to her grave every 14 May, are you? You should really move on.'

Now, you might be thinking: 'But it's different, you big fool. Visiting a grave doesn't involve hate, bitterness, malice or rancour. Building a commemorative statue doesn't either, and nor does placing flowers at the scene of a road accident.'

No, they don't. None of them do. They only involve *remembering, wanting to remember and asserting the importance of remembrance* in the context of something bad once having happened.

Those who follow the Grudge-fold Path (it might be just me at the moment, but that's fine — I'm happy to start small) understand that *the exact same principle can and should apply to grudge-holding.* History is history, whether it's personal or global/political, and history matters to most people. The past matters, because of the impact it's had on us and the light it can shine on the present and the future.

Imagine this: your teenage son's school suddenly announces that from now on, History lessons will not include any unpleasant or upsetting historical events. 'Dear Parents,' says the letter you receive, 'We're no longer going to be mentioning any wars, the Holocaust, Stalinism, Slavery, or the French Revolution in our teaching of History because all those things are, frankly, horrible. Instead, this term's History module will focus solely on nice things, like the time Mussolini gave his girlfriend Clara a beautiful bunch of flowers.' You would, quite rightly, think that the head teacher had gone completely bonkers. About devastating historical events and atrocities, we often say, 'Never forget'. Why? Is it that we want to extend the suffering for as long as possible? No, of course not. It's because we know that history (the horrible bits of it especially) contains useful lessons and warnings that we would be fools to ignore. Yet about upsetting personal incidents, we often hear people say, 'Don't hold a grudge. Move on, for your own sake.' Every time we say this, we are effectively asking someone to forget the important warnings and lessons from their own life history. Are we assuming that because it's personal, not political, it's not worthy of remembrance? I think so. I think that's exactly what we're doing.

'Hold on,' you may be thinking. 'No one is saying that we should forget important parts of our own life stories. But that's not the same thing as harbouring a grudge, is it?' This is true: it's not necessarily the same. I fondly remember my holiday at the Grand Hotel Tremezzo on Lake Como in the summer of 2017. That's not a grudge because there was nothing negative about the experience (apart from that the holiday ended, which I'm still not over). I also remember negative stories from my past that aren't grudges. I once had a terrible stomach upset while on an American book tour, but that's not a grudge because it might well not have been anyone's fault. If it *was* someone's fault – let's say a chef in a restaurant in New York didn't wash his hands properly and I got food poisoning as a result – then I don't know whose fault it was, and therefore can't hold a grudge about him. So that's not a grudge.

Anne Grey says: 'Honouring the past, valuing yourself for dealing with the challenges you've faced (whether you feel you've done this well or badly), developing wisdom and discernment – all of this is healthy and desirable.'

Adjectival Grudges

As part of my research for this book, I posted on social media the following question: 'Folks, what adjectives have people used about you that, whether they meant it meanly or not, you've never forgotten?' I asked the question because, quite out of the blue, someone on Twitter had told me in passing that I was 'scary'. I'm nearly 100 per cent certain that she wasn't trying to be rude or upset me; she presented the insult as if it wasn't one, as if it was simply a fact that I was scary and I was bound to think so too. Having spent a not insignificant chunk of my life being scared myself, of genuinely scary people – controlling, tyrannical, bullying, emotionally manipulative people – I was pretty surprised to think that anyone might see me as scary. I soon discovered that I wasn't the only person who'd ever baulked at a description of themselves. As soon as I'd asked the question, I was inundated with replies. Here are just some of the adjectival grudges I was sent:

The wife of a colleague, eyeing up what I was wearing, once called me a 'neat little man', and that has certainly stayed with me!

A rather famous theatre critic called me a 'stocky brunette' in the *Daily Telegraph*. The surrounding paragraph was fulsome in its praise but have NEVER forgotten or forgiven that adjective.

I was once described as aloof in a review at work. Which astounded me because I think I'm the most approachable person in the world, but my best friend confirmed that when I'm feeling shy I can indeed appear somewhat distant!

I was once described as 'so *Sound of Music*' by someone who apparently thought I needed to be more grounded.

My best friend at school described me as 'multifaceted', which I really warmed to until I found out much later that he meant that I was sly – i.e. worse than two-faced.

My daughter was called 'ruthlessly efficient' and still isn't sure whether it was a compliment or an insult.

Anne Grey says about these kind of adjectival grudges that you can 'see whatever has been said to you or about you as some kind of reflection of you. Some reflections are from a clear true mirror, some (maybe most) from a distorted mirror, but all are potentially helpful. For example, if someone describes you as dull then you have the opportunity to see how you can shine more brightly. This can be very freeing.

'If it's something like "you have a big nose" then you have the opportunity to love yourself even more, especially *because* of your beautiful big nose. Remember, always, that when someone is demeaning to others, it is they who are demeaned.'

I found the whole adjective experiment fascinating. I would define all of the above stories as grudges – negative experiences from the past that you choose to remember in the present for valid, positive reasons (such as reminding you never to be as rude or callous as X once was to you/reminding you you're so much better off without X in your life) – but I suspect many of the contributors here would not have sent them if I'd explicitly asked for grudges – because they wouldn't want to think of themselves as the grudge-holding type.

I really hope this book will change that. All we need to do is recognise grudges as a good thing and soon everyone will be proud to drag their secret stash out of the cupboard under the stairs and display them proudly in a new, shiny Grudge Cabinet in the best lounge.

If we want people to be proud of their grudges, we must immediately do two things:

1) Recognise that some people *already are* proud of their grudges. I am! If I am, then you can be too.
2) Create a new and better definition of grudges: one that doesn't involve never-ending feelings of hate, bitterness or rage; one that isn't inherently negative and that has

no stigma attached to it. We need a definition that
acknowledges that a grudge can and should be
something to welcome and celebrate.

I'm going to suggest a definition very shortly (it's actually mine,
the one I've been using for years, and I'm going to invite you
all to adopt it!) but first, let's get something potentially distracting
out of the way. Let's look at what is *not* a grudge . . .

What Isn't a Grudge?

Is this necessary? I mean, surely we all know what isn't a
grudge. A sunflower isn't a grudge, and neither is a tortoise.

The reason I'm going to tell you what *isn't* a grudge,
whether or not you think you need to be told, is that my
research for this book revealed a great degree of confusion
around the subject. I had many versions of this conversation,
with people who weren't all called Andrew:

ME: Do you have any grudges?

ANDREW: No, I don't think so. Why?

ME: I'm writing a book about grudges, so I'm
             kind of collecting them.

ANDREW: Oh. (*Looks worried. Wishes he could help me by
             supplying an anecdote for my book. Searches his
             memory.*) Well, last year my friend Priya

smashed my favourite coffee mug. Does that count?

ME: Have you held a grudge about it?

ANDREW: No, not at all. I'd almost forgotten it, in fact.

ME: Were you upset at the time?

ANDREW: No. I bought a replacement, exactly the same. And it was an accident – Priya got stung by a bee, and that's why she dropped the mug on the patio – so I wasn't annoyed at all.

ME: Okay . . . and did your view of Priya change in any way? Has the incident altered your thoughts or behaviour?

ANDREW: Not in the slightest.

ME: Then that's not a grudge. That's what I'd call: *not a grudge*. It's just a thing that happened.

Here's another example of Not a Grudge: every time Kate sees her grandmother in winter, Granny makes a comment about how inadequately dressed Kate is for the weather. She says things like, 'You must be freezing! Ooh, it makes me cold just to look at you! Haven't you got a warmer coat?

Why don't you put on tights?' Kate finds this infuriating, but she doesn't think any less of Granny, still loves her just as much and feels no need to remember or warn herself about this behaviour before she sees Granny the next time. In fact, *she totally wouldn't mind if she forgot entirely that Granny does this* – she would simply be irritated again the next time it happened, and then forget about it again. Her feelings towards Granny, her thoughts about her and her assessment of Granny as a safe and wholly good part of her life are exactly the same as they would be if Granny didn't make annoying comments about warm clothes.

Another Not-A-Grudge story is this: a close colleague once telephoned a relative of mine, without telling me, and told this relative he was worried about me because I was showing signs of getting involved with someone dangerous, and could she do something to stop me? (The person in question was and is highly unusual, but I had seen no evidence of danger; I have benefited *enormously* from having this person in my life, incidentally.) I was shocked that my colleague would try to involve a relative of mine, and made it clear I didn't think this was okay and didn't want it to happen again. I could see from my colleague's response that he *totally* understood how big a mistake he'd made. He said sorry in a heartfelt way, and ever since, he occasionally blurts out, 'I definitely *won't* be ringing your Aunt Mildred! Ha ha!' I know that his aim in saying this every so often is to reassure me that he *still* knows that he overstepped the mark. I don't feel I need a grudge about this because he saw and fully acknowledged his mistake, and it's never going to happen again.

If someone truly faces up to their mistake and is genuinely

sorry, I personally feel there is then no need to maintain a grudge. And if something is Not a Grudge, then you wouldn't mind if you forgot it completely. It has no continuing relevance or meaning in your life.

Here is the important point: *a Thing That Happens is not a grudge if it makes no intellectual, psychological or emotional impression, leaves no lasting residue of any kind and has no live charge in the present that you want or plan to take into the future.*

What Can and Should a Grudge Be?

There's a short and a long answer to this question. I'm going to save the more in-depth version for the end of the chapter, once I've taken you through all the reasoning, but let me give you the short answer right now:

A grudge is a true story from your past, involving a negative, hurtful or sub-optimal experience of some sort that it feels important to remember now and into the future.

A grudge doesn't have to be vengeful, all-consuming and bitter. In fact, it absolutely should not be any of these things once the initial emotional shock of the grudgee's transgression has worn off. Nobody benefits from continued anger and a lust for vengeance. That's why there are so many quotes of this sort to be found on the subject:

'To forgive is to set a prisoner free and discover that that prisoner was you' (Lewis B. Smedes, ethicist and theologian)

'Forgive others, not because they deserve forgiveness, but because you deserve peace' (widespread misquote of Jonathan Lockwood Huie)

'It is in pardoning that we are pardoned' (William Shakespeare)

'Resentment is like drinking poison and then hoping it will kill your enemies' (Has been variously attributed to Nelson Mandela, Gandhi, St Augustine, Buddha, Carrie Fisher and a random assortment of vicars)

All of the above quotes assume two premises:

1. that holding a grudge about somebody and not forgiving somebody are, and must be, the same thing.

2. that holding a grudge *necessarily* involves poisonous, turbulent or unpleasant feelings that do harm to the person feeling them.

Both of these assumptions are totally false. Couldn't be falser, in fact. It's possible, quite easily, to hold grudges happily. We don't have to be consumed by hatred and rage day after day, obsessing about our grudgee to the detriment of our work, family and personal hygiene. Have you ever heard someone say something like, 'Oh, I'm not angry any more – in fact,

I think it's hilarious, looking back – but I will never trust Sanjay again,' or 'I'm totally over it, but I certainly wouldn't put Debbie back on my Christmas card list'? I've heard that sort of comment many times, and I always interpret it as a sign that the speaker knows how to hold a grudge in a safe, responsible and positive way.

Sure, negative emotions are unavoidable, especially in the immediate aftermath of someone having wronged or wounded us, but we don't have to hard-bake them into our grudge. We should allow ourselves to feel all the emotions that arise naturally within us – and then let them pass. Very soon, the grudge we are left with has, or should have and certainly can have, nothing to do with negative emotions. It's simply a story we want to remember about a lesson learned; a story that has some significance for us.

Forgiving somebody means letting go of the negative emotions you have previously felt when thinking about them, or about what they did to you. It *does not* mean forcing your thoughts about them, or your behaviours around them, to be exactly the same as they were before the grudge-sparking incident or behaviour occurred. A lot of people think forgiveness ought to mean turning back the clock (impossible) and pretending the thing that happened never happened (possible, but silly. You might want to behave the same way towards that person afterwards – that's fine – but you can do that without trying to falsify history).

The trivial annoyances of life, like Granny telling Kate to put on a coat when she doesn't want to, do not require forgiveness. If a more serious transgression against you, or cause for hurt, takes place, you have five options:

1. Forgive (let go of the negative feelings attached to your thoughts about the person), hold no grudge and behave the same way to that person in future.

2. Forgive (let go of the negative feelings attached to your thoughts about the person), hold a grudge but behave the same way to that person in future. Only your thoughts have changed.

3. Forgive (let go of the negative feelings attached to your thoughts about the person), hold a grudge and behave differently to that person in future.

4. Don't forgive (hang on to the negative feelings attached to your thoughts about the person), hold a bad/wrong grudge and behave the same way to that person in future.

5. Don't forgive (hang on to the negative feelings attached to your thoughts about the person), hold a bad/wrong grudge and behave differently to that person in future.

We will look at bad, wrong and invalid kinds of grudges in Chapter 9. For our present purposes, all you need to know is that if you're hanging on for too long to negative feelings like bitterness or hate, and winding them around your decision to hold a grudge, then your grudge is currently unprocessed and not doing you or anyone else any good. It might even be dangerous. I will talk you through how to process your grudges and make them safe and good in Chapter 8.

Out of the five options above, only two are good/correct. If someone significantly mistreats you and you follow the course of action detailed in answer number 1, then you are not taking the mistreatment of yourself sufficiently seriously. There's only one kind of transgression/hurt for which number 1 is the correct procedure. Can you guess what it is? We've talked about it already. It's the hurt you feel in a situation where Someone Has Done Nothing Wrong. (Remember Aunt Doreen, who moved in next door to you without asking you how you'd feel about it?) For genuine transgressions – where someone has done something to you or those you care about – answers 2 and 3 are the correct choices. And you can see from the difference between them that your behaviour towards your grudgee does not need to change – not one jot. Only your thoughts about them need to change.

A grudge is, and should be, something lasting but not necessarily obtrusive or constant, and definitely not something rage-inducing, debilitating or harmful – which is why 4 and 5 above are terrible choices. Most of my grudges were things I thought about very rarely. (Obviously this changed when I started planning to write this book!) Some I enjoyed and found quite hilarious – I pulled them out of my Grudge Cabinet every so often and admired them. 'What a fine specimen!' I thought to myself.

I wouldn't want to be without any of my grudges. Each one is an important lesson I've learned from my own life story. None of them involves a shred of anger or unhappiness (though I might have felt those feelings in the immediate aftermath of the sparking incident), and I've never cut anyone out of my life or wreaked a terrible revenge (or even a puny, mild one). Any grudge that leads to a revenge-act or even revenge-planning is a dangerous grudge and should be deactivated immediately. (See Chapter 8 for more details.) Good grudges that harm neither the holder nor the grudgee, on the other hand, are part of a balanced and healthy psychological diet.

We hold grudges when all of the things listed below apply:

1. a negative or hurtful incident or behaviour occurs.

2. we know, or think we know, who (individual or group) is responsible.

3. we decide we want to remember this because remembering it feels important to us – maybe we're going to learn a lesson from it, or maybe it changes who we are from that moment on, or it made us feel such strong feelings when it happened that it would be personal-history vandalism to allow ourselves to forget it – it would feel like the psychological equivalent of tearing down St Paul's Cathedral or spray-painting over the Mona Lisa. We define it to ourselves and/or others as a grudge.

There are many different ways we might express what a grudge is. My friend Hilary, when asked for a definition, said, 'Oh, a grudge is when something from ages ago is Still A Thing – capital letters. It might have happened years ago, but you know it'll never be Not A Thing.' This is what I mean when I talk about a live charge. A past incident that has a live charge (of relevance, not of anger or pain) in the present is Still A Thing.

Hilary's daughter, Ayesha, has a friend, Claire, who went through a three-month phase of being startlingly horrible to her. This phase started when Ayesha got her first boyfriend. Claire suddenly felt left out, though she in fact spent far more time with Ayesha than the new boyfriend did. Ayesha and Hilary dealt with the problem and the behaviour stopped. Ayesha is still officially best friends with Claire in the eyes of the world, is still very nice to her and has never retaliated in any way, but she also has a grudge about Claire. She told Hilary, 'I was totally going to ask her to be maid of honour or chief bridesmaid when I get married. Now I definitely won't. As long as I have to see her, I'm going to behave well towards her and be friendly, but once we leave college and I don't *have* to see her, I won't keep in touch with her. I wouldn't ever feel fully safe again around her. Anyone who can react so shittily to their best friend getting a boyfriend isn't a true friend.'

An interesting little postscript to that story is this: Ayesha found out that Claire had been complaining to her about how she is going to be bored all of this summer, because she's got nothing to do. Asked 'Won't you be hanging around with Ayesha?', Claire replied, 'Nah, she's only interested in hanging around with her boyfriend these days.' The truth is that Ayesha plans to see her boyfriend during the summer holidays, but she also plans to hang out with her new close friends Ella and Juan. She started to cultivate their friendship when Claire started being spiteful to her. Claire might blame Ayesha's romantic relationship for their friendship not being what it used to be, when in fact the *only* thing that has led to Ayesha and Claire being less close is that Claire started to attack Ayesha as soon as she got a boyfriend.

Can a Grudge Turn Into Not a Grudge?

Absolutely! My grudge about my colleague who rang Aunt Mildred was a Grudge that is now Not a Grudge. We can't, shouldn't and mustn't assume that we will hold all of our grudges for ever. Here are some reasons why we might discontinue a grudge:

1. The grudgee apologises in a way that indicates they truly get it, are remorseful and won't behave in a similar way again.

2. You realise that you were wrong to hold the grudge in the first place. It was invalid, bad or wrong.

3. You become aware that the grudge – organically, and of its own accord – simply isn't there any more. You forget it, or it loses its live charge.

4. The grudge story you thought was fully told turns out not to be, and continues in the present in a way that affects your desire or ability to hold a grudge. An example: I wrote a book featuring a noisy neighbour, 'Mr Fahrenheit', so named because he regularly played 'Don't Stop Me Now' by Queen loudly at one in the morning. At the time, I had an occasionally noisy next-door neighbour. Some while after my book was published, I noticed that this neighbour had given his house a name and etched this name into the glass above the front door for all to see. The name is still there

now, and will possibly be the name of that house for ever: Farron Heights. When I first saw it, I laughed for about three hours. My grudge about my neighbour's noise-making vanished on the spot. I felt as if, by naming his house Farron Heights, he was inviting me to join in with a joke that linked his noisiness to my book. Weirdly, I felt as if it was a kind of peace offering. It's possible I was quite wrong and his intention was to piss me off, but I simply couldn't maintain the grudge after seeing that name carved into the glass above his door. I appreciated the way he had entered into the imaginative world of my book!

5. The grudgee does something else, later, that you feel cancels out the original incident. If, for example, you have a grudge about Gemma who forgot your birthday two years running (which you took as evidence that she doesn't care about you) and then, out of the blue, Gemma drives all the way from Plymouth to Aberdeen to deliver you an amazing present at Christmas, you might well decide that she obviously does care, and drop your missed-birthdays grudge.

In my first draft of this list, I also had: 6) the grudgee dies/ leaves your life and you're sure you'll never see or be affected by them again. I struck that one off the list because your grudge about Terence might well still be valid and have a live charge even after Terence's death – for instance, it might teach you the valuable lesson, 'Steer clear of gits like Terence, always.'

If a grudge is causing you any sort of stress or discomfort, then it is either an unprocessed, bad or invalid grudge. We will deal with these later. For now, I'm going to focus on their opposite: good grudges. *By this, I do not mean remembering good things that happen.* (In a later chapter I'm going to advise you to do precisely that, but we're going to call those positive-live-charge-stories by a different name.) By 'good grudges', I mean: valid grudges that you are correct and wise to hold, held in a wise and correct manner.

Here's the more in-depth answer to the question 'What should a grudge be?' A grudge should be:

1. a story about something that happened in the past (whether ten years or two seconds ago) . . .

2. that you don't want to forget. You want to hold onto it, and 'bookmark' it in your mind . . .

3. because there is an important lesson in it, or a signpost for you – something you do or don't want to be or do, and you want to use this grudge story to reinforce your resolve . . .

4. or the grudge story might powerfully remind you of a value that you hold dear . . .

5. and it will also contain a new opinion or new thoughts, formed since the grudge-sparking incident took place, about the grudgee (which might be as simple as: 'She did X that one time, which means I now don't trust her as much', which will link to whatever thoughts you have now about her doing X then) . . .

6. and it might also contain new, changed behaviour towards that person.

7. It shouldn't contain anger, bitterness, rage, hate or any of those other unpleasant feelings listed at the start of this chapter. We might feel any or all of these when the incident happens and for a while afterwards, but these feelings should be in a different compartment from our grudge story if we want to hold a good grudge. Good grudges can't be contaminated by angry feelings and negative energy.

8. Good grudges *should* make us feel something, however. They should make us feel empowered; wiser; sometimes entertained, if there's a humorous aspect to the story. Most of all, they should make us feel that the thing that happened to us, the sparking incident, matters in the world. In this sense, grudges (like the grey marble plinth for the murdered window cleaners) are commemorative items. I'm going to say this again in bold because it's really crucial: **if someone harms you, that matters not only to you but also in the world.** The moment you tell yourself that your ill-treatment should or does matter only to you, you're on the way to accepting a world in which no one cares about anyone else. When someone tells you 'Move on, it's not worth holding a grudge' immediately after you've told them about Pauline who just dropped sheep poo into your breakfast cereal when she thought you weren't looking, what they're actually saying is, 'The fact that you've been treated atrociously doesn't matter to me at all, and

I'd like it if you would agree that it doesn't matter to you either, because then we can both stop thinking about your needs, rights and feelings.' Therefore (wow, number 8 turned out to be pretty long!) your grudges should make you feel that you have something to commemorate what happened and acknowledge its importance.

Anne Grey says, 'I agree that it matters when people harm us. Acting out of love, wisdom and compassion for ourselves and others is the key to a better world.'

In the next chapter, we're going to look at the many different kinds of grudges, but first it's time for one of my favourite grudge stories. This is a 1-carat grudge anecdote. I'll introduce you to my carat-based grudge grading system a little later on, but for the time being, all you need to know is that a 1-carat grudge is the least grudgeworthy (in the opinion of the grudge-holder) kind of grudge a person can hold. If someone burned down your house, deliberately laying waste to your collection of Agatha Christie paperbacks, that certainly would *not* be only a 1-carat, for example. So what might a 1-carat grudge look like?

The Taxi That Didn't Move

I'd like to introduce you to my fictitious godmother, Fern, and her husband, Vern. About twelve years ago, my husband went away for a few days and, while he was away, Fern and Vern came to visit. They had previously made comments that suggested they felt I might be in some way not okay without my husband at home, which wasn't at all the case; I was absolutely fine.

I lived in a house that had an unusual front door: a 'stable' style door with two separate parts. It did not – *could* not – close and stay closed unless bolted from the inside or locked with an actual key from the outside.

My kids were three and one at the time, so they were tucked up in bed asleep before Fern, Vern and I had dinner. We had a lovely meal and a great evening, and then Fern called a taxi to take her and Vern to the train station.

When it arrived, and Fern and Vern started to put on their coats, I remembered that I needed to go outside too; I'd left some papers I needed in the boot of my car, which was parked in the driveway, about six or seven feet from the house. I said to Fern and Vern, 'I'll come out with you – I've got to get something from the car.'

Vern immediately looked very concerned. 'Oh,' he said, frowning as if this was bad news. 'Well, why don't you go and get it now? We'll wait here.'

I couldn't work out what the problem was. 'There's no need to wait,' I said. 'We can all go out together.'

'But you might get locked out of the house if the front door swings shut, and then the children will be trapped in the house on their own,' said Vern. 'If they wake up and need you, and you can't get back in . . .'

'Oh! Don't worry,' I told him. 'It's physically impossible for that to happen.' I explained why, and offered to show Vern the front door so that he could see for himself. He said no, he didn't want to look at the door. What he wanted, he explained, was for me to agree to his original suggestion: he and Fern wait in the house while I go and get my papers from the car, and then they leave after I've come back inside.

I could have made my life a little easier by agreeing to this, however crazy it was, but I was annoyed. Vern was being ridiculous. Just in case anyone missed the key point here: it was *impossible* for my front door to shut by accident. And apart from anything else, even if Vern didn't believe me about the mechanics of my own door, what did he imagine I would do if I *did* find myself accidentally locked out of my house? Shrug, say, 'Oh, well, I guess the kids'll have to fend for themselves' and swan off to a hotel for the night? In those circumstances, what I would do – what anyone intelligent who cared about their kids would do – is go to a neighbour's house, phone a 24-hour emergency locksmith and make sure to get back into the house as soon as possible. If, before the locksmith arrived, I'd heard the sound of children screaming or seen flames rising, I'd have smashed a window and entered the house that way.

I didn't say any of this to Vern. I decided he was neurotic enough without me mentioning screams and flames. I simply said, 'You're not going to wait here till I come back in. We're all going to go out together.'

So we did. Vern and Fern went and got into their taxi, which was parked on the street, across the entrance to my driveway. I went to my car, opened the boot and found the papers I needed. (This took a while; the boot of my car is usually not the tidiest place in the world.) I then locked the car and was about to go back into the house through the wide-open front door when I noticed something: the taxi that was supposed to be taking Fern and Vern to the station had not moved an inch.

I wondered if there was a problem. Then I heard Vern snap at the driver, 'No. We're *not* going to the station. Not yet. Stay where you are.'

I stared at Vern through the taxi window. He stared back. It was at that moment that the terrible truth struck me: he was going to make the taxi driver wait there, in the street, until he saw me go back inside the house and close the front door.

To give myself time to strategise, I opened my car's boot again and pretended to be looking for something else. This is what ran through my mind while I was rummaging around in search of the made-up thing I didn't need:

1. This is a terrible boundary violation.

2. No it isn't. Vern's paying for the taxi, and it's parked on a public road, not on your property. Vern has every right to sit there in his taxi for as long as he wants, as long as he's willing to pay the driver for his time – and that's between the two of them.

3. Okay, in strict legal terms, he's doing nothing wrong but . . . it's still ridiculously creepy.

4. No fucking way am I letting him win. I'll staying out here all night if I have to, with the front door wide open.

5. Much as I don't want Vern to win, I really don't want to stay out here all night. It's cold and I've got stuff to do.

6. I know! I've got a cunning plan . . .

I went back inside and closed the front door. A few minutes later I went back outside to see if the taxi had moved. It had; it was gone. And then . . . (I'm wondering if anyone can guess what I did next. What would you have done next?)

Here's what I wish I'd done next: waited until I knew that Fern and Vern were on the train and couldn't possibly come back, and then texted Vern the following message: 'You know when you were in the taxi and I was standing next to my car? Did you by any chance see me drop anything? I've lost an important document. I'm out here searching for it in the car right now, but it's not here, and nor is it on the driveway.' Vern would have known that *I'd* won and he'd lost: I was outside my house again, unsupervised by him this time, and there wouldn't have been a damn thing he could do about it. Wouldn't that have been brilliant? Pity I only thought of it five minutes before writing this paragraph.

Here's what I actually did next: I poured myself a glass of wine, sat down and literally shook for the next ten minutes or so. I paced up and down, drinking, thinking 'An awful thing has happened!' and 'That was terrible!' It wasn't anger I felt (anger can be energising and even quite good fun). No, it was a much more sickened, violated feeling. Accompanying this was the conviction that I had just witnessed a vote of no confidence in my ability to look after myself, my house and my children in a proper way.

About half an hour later, I went outside and stood on my driveway and thought, 'Fuck you, Vern. Fuck you and your stupid taxi and your stupid train.' Then I went back inside.

My anger had disappeared by the next morning, as had the sickened/violated feeling. What hadn't disappeared was my new awareness that Vern was an irrational, neurotic control freak – and it was that new knowledge that I used to fashion my 1-carat grudge. After that night, I took steps to ensure that I was always with my husband when Vern came round. I knew that Vern was less likely to worry that my children might come to harm if I wasn't the sole parent in charge (I don't know if this was sexism on his part or just a conviction that I'm too crap to look after anything/anyone properly) and so it seemed a sensible step if I wanted to minimise the chances of Vern behaving that way in the future.

I don't know how serious you think this grudge ought to be, but in case anyone's wondering why it gets the lowest possible carat rating, it's because:

1. Vern meant no harm. All he wanted was to ensure my children weren't left unattended.

2. In certain moods, Vern is a deeply irrational catastrophist and can't help it. As a child, his home life was, in some ways, unstable. So it stands to reason that Vern might have some irrational fears in relation to the well-being of children.

3. Nothing bad actually happened to me or anyone else. I was annoyed and shaken, but I wasn't maimed, slandered, punched or dunked in a bucket of fish guts. I wasn't emotionally scarred, and my confidence in my parenting abilities wasn't dented, in spite of Vern's behaviour.

This grudge is one of my favourites because it's so absurd and hilarious. I love telling this story to people, and I laugh every time I think about it – especially the part where I go outside and stand on my driveway for a few minutes, purely to prove that I can do that whenever the hell I want to.

3

The Many Different
Kinds of Grudge

'I hold grudges, but I can't hate nobody, that's not my nature.'

Notorious B.I.G.

The world of grudges is a rich and colourful one, my friends! There are many exotic and unusual varieties, and in this chapter I'm going to introduce you to some of them. I won't talk here about the various wrong or invalid types of grudge – I'll get onto those later. For the time being, let's stick to the good grudges, of which, it turns out, there are many different species. Since no one has ever undertaken a comprehensive analysis of grudges before, I have taken on the role of pioneering grudge classifier and created what I hope is a kind of periodic table, but for grudges instead of chemical elements.

When I asked my husband how he would classify grudges, he looked puzzled and said that he wouldn't. 'What about if you had to?' I said.

'I don't know,' he said. 'I might have grudges against people as one type, and then grudges against places—'

'No, that's not the best way to do it!' I cut him off, excited by the idea I'd just had. He shrugged and left the room (possibly holding a grudge because I'd insisted he participate in a conversation he didn't want to have, and then talked over him).

My idea, prompted by his suggested classification system, was that the most meaningful way to sort grudges was by psychological theme or gist, and so that's what I've done. I've referred to some already: 'Right Thing, Too Late', for example – a name that explains not what happened in the particular spark-incident story, but *why* you're holding that grudge.

Listed below are twenty common grudge types. Some grudges will fit into more than one of these categories – quite a few, in fact. There are many, many more types that I haven't included here, and these will be added to the 'How To Hold a Grudge' page of my website as a regular weekly feature. (If you can think of any varieties that I might not know about, please do email me at grudgescanbegood@gmail.com!)

For each grudge type listed here, I've given a brief example. All are true stories.

1) UNPROVOKED ATTACK GRUDGE

This is a simple one, and self-explanatory.

Example

It's Rebecca's fortieth birthday, and she's invited two friends, Carol and Sonia, out for dinner. Rebecca and Sonia live on the same street, so they agree to travel to the restaurant together in Sonia's car, and Carol will meet them there. During the drive to the restaurant, Sonia and Rebecca catch up on all the news and gossip. At the restaurant, they meet Carol, who says happy birthday to Rebecca and asks what presents she got for her birthday. Sonia then asks Carol how she is, and spends ten minutes talking to Carol about her news. Rebecca listens, not joining in. Then Rebecca suddenly bursts into tears and storms out of the restaurant.

Later, when Rebecca reappears at the table, red-eyed, and Carol and Sonia ask her why she was upset, Rebecca says, aggressively, 'You've *ruined* my birthday, both of you. Completely ruined it! Sonia, you started speaking to Carol at the restaurant and the two of you completely ignored me, even though you knew it was my birthday.' Sonia replies that she simply asked Carol the same 'How are you? What have you been up to?' questions that she'd asked Rebecca during their drive to the restaurant, and that there is nothing wrong with her doing that, even on Rebecca's birthday. Rebecca disagrees. She says, 'It's *my* birthday dinner. You and Carol shouldn't have been having a conversation that didn't involve me.'

Frighteningly, this is a true story. Rebecca's attack on Sonia and Carol was completely unprovoked, and therefore grudge-worthy. Interestingly, Sonia and Carol responded very differently when the birthday-ruining accusation was levelled at them. Carol said, 'What? Are you mental? Fuck off, I'm not having that. That's insane!' before storming out of the restaurant herself. The next day, Rebecca rang her and apologised. Carol forgave her and did not hold a grudge. Carol and Rebecca are still good friends. Sonia said nothing, and gave Rebecca a lift home, during which journey Rebecca listed all the other times that Sonia and Carol had behaved as if they preferred each other to Rebecca (none of which was true).

After dropping Rebecca off at her house with a friendly smile, Sonia went home and thought about what had happened. She decided she did not want someone capable of this sort of unprovoked attack in her life, and so cut Rebecca off altogether. Four years later, she relented and spoke to Rebecca at a mutual friend's wedding, after which they resumed their friendship. Some years after that, when drunk, Rebecca brought up the birthday dinner incident again and said, jokily, 'I shouldn't have reacted the way I did, but come on – you did act like a bit of a fucker, didn't you?' Sonia didn't know if Rebecca was referring to the original incident or to her shunning of Rebecca for four years. Either way, Sonia found it interesting that Rebecca saw her as being at fault.

2) UNREASONABLE IMPOSITION GRUDGE (A.K.A. ATTEMPTED TIME-THEFT GRUDGE)

This is when someone tries to impose on you and puts you in the awkward position of having to say no to a request that should never have been made of you in the first place. (I know, I know: we should all be able to say no, without explanation or guilt, whenever we want to – but in reality, many of us do and always will feel awkward and guilty about doing so, which is why it remains important not to impose unreasonably upon others.)

Serena and Pauline are colleagues of sorts, as they are both freelancers in the same industry, and sometimes meet at conferences, where they get on.

Serena is bossy. She likes to get her way wherever possible. On the plus side, she is energetic and her organisational capabilities are legendary. If Serena says it will get done, then it's done, and most often to perfection. Another thing about Serena that is easy to miss (because you're distracted by her bright, efficient, bossy side) is her kindness. It's not just a general kindness of the sort that most decent people pride themselves on, but the sort that allows her to go off and look after her very sick sister. Pauline liked to think she'd do the same if she had had a sister, and was impressed by Serena's saintly behaviour.

One of Serena's best friends was a woman called Cassie. Cassie was one of those people to whom bad things constantly happen. And whenever they did, there was Serena, ready to pick up the pieces. After each disastrous turn of events visits would ensue, or, when she couldn't visit, Serena and Cassie would talk for hours on the phone or on Skype.

This was the situation when Pauline moved into the same village as Cassie, into a house just across the road. Pauline had not met Cassie before, but since she was such a dear friend of Serena's, Pauline decided to pay her a visit. She introduced herself and invited Cassie over for coffee. Pauline liked Cassie, and still does – but in a very limited way. Almost at once, she discovered that Cassie lived in a situation of almost unimaginable physical chaos. Her house was one where you didn't really want to sit down, it was so filthy. This, coupled with the disastrous state of her personal life, made Pauline want to run a mile. Pauline wants nothing more than a tidy life, so resolved to have as little do with Cassie as she possibly could, and only to interact with her when absolutely necessary in her own home or a neutral environment.

One day, Pauline tells me, she received a long email from Serena, telling her that Cassie was going through a really hard time and because she, Serena, was going to be out of the country for six weeks, could Pauline please undertake to look after Cassie in her absence? Check on her every day to see she was okay, be there for her to go to when she felt at the end of her tether and so on.

The request shocked Pauline. By writing in this way, Serena was assuming that Pauline was like her: self-abnegating, as close to Cassie as she was, ready to drop everything and run at the mere sign of distress to help someone she hardly knew and whom she had resolved to avoid. She said no; she tried to say it gently but it was a very definite 'no'. Serena immediately wrote back saying, 'No worries' and that was that, but Pauline still bears a grudge against her for putting her in the position of being The Unkind One: the one who wouldn't stir herself to help a woman living just across the road, a heartless person who didn't help in times of trouble. Pauline's biggest grudge is this: many of their mutual acquaintances who must have heard this story will also have cast her as cruel and unfeeling and she resents Serena for that – and for not understanding that it was more than presumptuous to assume that Pauline would be ready to drop everything to care for someone who was a friend of *hers*.

3) ILL-JUDGED JOKE GRUDGE

They might have been only joking, but who cares? A joke can still be bang out of order, or they might have been 'kidding on the square' – telling a joke that also happens to reflect the truth – to avoid repercussions.

Example
Melissa spent quite a lot of money hiring a large, beautiful house where the whole extended family could meet for a special occasion. All branches of the family came, and Melissa's uncle brought his newish girlfriend, Xanthe. At a certain point in the celebrations, Melissa nipped out for an hour or so to walk her dog. When she returned to the hired house and rang the bell, Xanthe opened the door and said, 'Not today, thanks!' in a bright voice, then slammed the door in Melissa's face.

It was a joke. A few seconds later, Xanthe opened the door and said, 'Haha – come in.' She meant no harm, but Melissa has disliked her ever since.

4) BETRAYAL OF TRUST/DISHONESTY GRUDGE

Another very simple one: when someone lies to you, shatters your trust in them or breaks a promise they made to you.

Example
Jenny, Susan and Fay were best friends as teenagers, and went everywhere together: an inseparable trio. Aged fourteen, they made a pact: that they would tell each other (but no one

else) when each of them first had sex. Two years later, Susan had sex with her boyfriend Simon, and told Jenny and Fay. Susan believed that she was the first of the three to sleep with a boyfriend. Fay immediately looked at Jenny in a knowing way, with a grin, and said, 'Shall I tell her?' Jenny looked deeply uncomfortable. Susan knew, immediately, what was coming. Fay said, 'Actually, I slept with Neil six months ago. Sorry, I know I said I'd tell you, but I was worried about what you'd think. I only told Jenny, because I didn't think she'd disapprove.' Susan held a grudge against Fay – for breaking the promise that they would all tell each other, and for lying about her true reason. Susan knew the true reason Fay had told Jenny and not her was to create a bond with Jenny and exclude Susan.

Revealing to Susan not only that she'd slept with Neil but also that Jenny had known and kept the secret was, in Susan's view, a clear attempt to cause a rift between Jenny and Susan so that Fay could have Susan all to herself. Susan didn't give Fay what she wanted. She didn't hold a grudge against Jenny, recognising that Fay had put her in an impossible position, and the three of them remained 'best friends'. Susan never again really liked or trusted Fay, but she kept this quiet in order not to upset Jenny, who did still like Fay. Once they all left high school, Susan didn't keep in touch with Fay.

Thirty years later, Fay found Susan's Facebook page and sent her a friendly email saying 'Hi! How are you? It'd be great to hear from you.' Susan debated whether or not to reply. Fay had regularly behaved badly when Susan had known her, and Susan didn't feel inclined to renew any sort of acquaintance with Fay.

5) HYPOCRISY GRUDGE

This is the grudge you hold when people have one rule for themselves and one for other people.

Example
Karen's best friend Audrey is constantly posting things on social media along the lines of 'Kindness costs nothing' and 'Be kind – everyone you meet is fighting a hard battle that you know nothing about'. But whenever Karen disappoints Audrey in any way, Audrey turns on her and becomes very spiteful. And she never stops to think how absurd it is that she does all that posting about love and kindness, but then whenever someone annoys her in real life, she quickly turns vicious. Karen holds a substantial grudge about this.

6) 'PEOPLE OF THE LIE' (POTL) GRUDGE

This is one of the most important grudge types – because the events that create POTL grudges are among the most morally serious of transgressions. If you have several, or even one POTL grudge against a particular person, it's advisable to think very carefully about what protective steps you need to take, for yourself and those around you, if you're going to continue to allow this person to be part of your life.

First, let me explain the name, which is the title of a brilliant book (with one extremely peculiar supernatural chapter at the end, but apart from that chapter it's an ace book) by psychotherapist M. Scott Peck. Peck argues that the people who deserve to be labelled evil are not necessarily those who have done the most harmful or despicable deeds. Peter might, for instance, murder his wife Margery and their two children in a jealous rage, and then say, 'Oh, my God, what have I done? What terrible deed have I done? Strike me down for my unforgivable crime!' Peck argues that, if someone like Peter responds to his own evil behaviour in this way – by recognising his own culpability and not seeking to minimise his wrongdoing – then there is hope for him. He is not necessarily an evil person. The people to whom the word 'evil' can reasonably be applied, Peck claims, are those who believe they are innately and inherently good and therefore incapable of doing anything bad. This means that when they attack or harm someone, since their starting point is 'I am wholly good, always in the right, and only do good things', they have to arrange the narrative in their mind so that the person they've harmed is in fact the bad one. To Peck, the warped dishonesty of this outlook justifies the label 'evil', and he believes these are the people who do the most harm in the world.

Example
To illustrate what a POTL grudge might look like, I'm deliberately going to use a fairly low-stakes example from my personal experience. Despite the low stakes, the incident chilled me because I could see that, in a high-stakes situation, that same person behaving in this same way might do grave damage.

A group of us (between twenty and thirty people) are all customers of the same business. It's a business that encourages communication among its customers, and so we have a group email thread that enables us all to communicate with each other. I hadn't been entirely satisfied for some time with parts of the service this business provides, but I was always too busy to do anything about it, and I kept telling myself I'd deal with it later. But I felt ripped off. One day, another customer on the email thread wrote to us all and said, 'Just wondering, guys, are any of you unhappy about the lack of A, B and C?' They were all things I was unhappy about, so I pressed 'Reply all' and said yes, A, B and C were all things that, contractually, this business is obliged to provide to its customers, and it wasn't providing those things at the moment.

It wasn't just me, it turned out. Many of us wrote on the group thread saying, yes, the business was not giving us the service it ought to be providing. We agreed that we would draft a letter that we could all sign, respectfully and politely pointing out that the business had promised us certain things, that they were currently not providing these things and please could they make sure that, in future, these things are provided? There was no anger, no recriminations, only people quite reasonably wanting to be furnished with some basic elements of the thing they'd been promised, and were paying lots of money for, that were currently lacking.

Some in the group thread remained silent. I assumed the silent ones were the People Who Are Terrified Of Everything Even Slightly Contentious. In any group, there are always some who fall into this category. My mum once said to me something I've never forgotten. She said, 'You have to remember: most people are scared of most things.' I think this is absolutely true, and I imagined that the people who weren't saying anything were staying silent because they feared that the business would wreak a terrible vengeance upon them if they signed the group letter.

While this was going on, my daughter's social life brought her into contact with a boy whose mother was one of the customers receiving the group-thread emails. She hadn't replied and didn't intend to, he told my daughter. Then he added, with an air of disdain, 'She told me that she doesn't want to be part of the stirring.'

Consciously or unconsciously, the boy's mother was trying to portray what those of us asking for better treatment were doing as a negative and trouble-causing initiative and us as all being trouble-stirring killjoys, creating negativity in the world. That teenage boy was led to believe that the people who say, 'Please can you give us what you promised to give us when we paid you?' are the bad guys in this situation, and his mother, who is not 'being part of the stirring', is the noble one emitting positive energy. In fact, his mother is a Person of the Lie.

A People of the Lie (POTL) grudge is a grudge you hold when someone pretends to be a good person resisting bad things, and in fact they are the opposite: a bad person resisting good things.

7) UNDERESTIMATION GRUDGE

When someone unfairly underestimates you.

Example
When I was nine, my teacher told our class that there was a national poetry competition for children coming up, and she

wanted us all to write a poem so that she could enter them in the competition. We did. Writing poetry was my favourite hobby, and I was good at it, at least for someone my age. I could do rhyme and form, but I had no idea about how not to be pretentious and grandiose. One verse of my poem went like this:

Remember when the sea was blue?
'Tis now a devil shade of red.
(something something something something – I don't
    remember line 3, but I'm sure it was equally
    cringeworthy)
The trees are shrivelled now, and dead.

My teacher read the poems that I and my classmates had written, and announced that she would submit them all for the competition apart from mine. She asked me to stay behind after school. I was baffled. Once all the other children had left, she told me that she wasn't going to enter my poem because I obviously hadn't written it myself; I couldn't possibly have written such a good poem at my age, so I must have cheated. She tried to browbeat me into 'confessing' but I didn't – I couldn't, because I'd written every word myself.

The next day, my parents came into school to stick up for me, armed with several notebooks full of other poems I'd written, which were equally embarrassing but prosodically proficient. Still the teacher wouldn't back down. In the end she agreed to a compromise: if I sat and wrote a poem in front of her, under exam conditions, she would enter that in the competition. I did, and she did. My poem didn't win.

My original poem that I'd wanted to enter probably wouldn't have won either, but I thought it was much better than the one I'd been forced to write to prove I wasn't a cheat and a liar.

Connected: A close cousin of the Underestimation Grudge is the Fake Underestimation or Denial of Credit/Achievement Grudge. Many years later, when I was an adult and had published some poetry books, one of my poetry collections was shortlisted for an award. A relative asked me, 'Which one of the judges do you know?' She wasn't joking. She knew perfectly well that I didn't know any of the judges. When I told her that I didn't, she said, 'Oh. Oh, right. Sorry.' She *wanted* me to believe that she had assumed I couldn't possibly have been shortlisted without a friend on the judging panel.

Any grudge from this 'family' of grudges – the Underestimation family – can be a powerful motivating force. Many of us are spurred on to do great things by the under-estimation and withheld praise and recognition of others.

8) POLITICAL GRUDGE

When you have a grudge about someone on account of their political views or behaviour around political issues.

Examples (an assortment, for political balance!)
Jasper holds a grudge against meat eaters. He believes they are deliberately ignoring the ethical and environmental impact of consuming animal-based products: with every steak, he says, at least 100 gallons of water are wasted and the deforestation of the rainforest is accelerated.

Danni's grudge is against the UK government, who, in her opinion, penalise disabled people by cutting their benefits.

Colleen has a massive grudge against her husband who has kept his UK Labour Party membership, even after the party came under the control of people Colleen believes to be terrorrist-supporting Stalinists. She now considers her husband to be a colluder with evil (though she concedes that he sees the situation very differently).

Claire's sister is a Donald Trump supporter. Claire, a committed feminist, thinks Trump is a misogynist, and so she will never forgive her sister.

Miranda is a passionate fan of Jordan Peterson – psychology professor and bestselling author of the self-help book *12 Rules For Life*. She believes Peterson is a strong force for good and wisdom in the world, and has a grudge about all her left-wing friends who behave as if Peterson represents the forces of darkness.

9) LACK OF SUPPORT GRUDGE

You'd hold this grudge when someone failed to support you in a way that hurt or disappointed you.

Example
Jenna was one of a group of seven close friends for many years. One of these friends, Barbara, was always making

tactless remarks, designed to attack Jenna's confidence in her own appearance. Each one, on its own, was a little throwaway comment that could have possibly been explained away, but the regularity with which she did it made it absolutely clear to Jenna that she meant to hurt and undermine her.

One time she was describing a woman as ugly and, immediately afterwards, she said to Jenna, 'I mean, she's *much* uglier than you, Jenna,' as if she was giving her a compliment. After ten years of this treatment, Jenna wrote to Barbara asking her if she could please stop doing this – stop regularly insulting her, stop making carefully designed snide remarks. Jenna explained that she still wanted Barbara in her life, but that she couldn't continue to see her if the passive-aggressive remarks didn't stop.

Barbara denied everything and accused Jenna of attacking her unfairly – and so Jenna felt she had to cut Barbara out of her life. She knew deep down that Barbara was not a good, safe or nice person, so she was no great loss. What hurt Jenna – and what she held a grudge about – was that not one of the other five people in their friendship group ever said to her, 'I know Barbara *did* do that to you and she was wrong to do it.' None of the five ever validated the fact that Jenna had been regularly attacked by Barbara in this way for more than a decade. It felt to Jenna as if they all agreed that she was making a fuss about nothing. Jenna is still friends with them all, but if they ever need her support in a situation where they're the ones being attacked, she might not rush to provide it.

10) LACK OF CARE GRUDGE

This is similar to number 9, but also a bit different. Care and support are not quite the same thing.

Example
Dawn was doing some work for a particular organisation and had agreed to do three things in order to publicise this work. She received a call from the PR firm the organisation was using to promote this initiative, asking her if she could do an additional, fourth thing: an interview for a Sky channel that would have to be recorded at six the following morning. She was feeling very unwell at the time, with a terrible cold/ cough/sore throat bug, so she said, 'I'm really sorry, I just can't. I'm doing a big event tonight that might finish late and I'm ill, and if I get up at four-thirty in the morning, I'll only make myself iller.'

Instead of replying, as anyone decent would, with, 'Of course, we completely understand,' this PR firm kept ringing and trying to change Dawn's mind. Over and over again, different people from the firm would call. When Dawn stopped answering the calls, they started texting her, over and over.

Dawn texted back with, 'I understand that this is important to you, but please can you try to understand that I am feeling very ill and can barely face doing this evening's event, let alone an additional one tomorrow morning? I cannot do it. Sorry.' But they kept texting her and pleading with her to change her mind, until she rang the head of the organisation she was doing the work for and asked them to contact the PR agency and forbid anyone from there from ever contacting her again.

Dawn made the decision that she would never work with this PR firm again under any circumstances. In her view this demonstration of lack of care for the well-being of another person merits a forever grudge. She also has a grudge about the organisation, who continued to work with that PR company, even knowing how they had treated Dawn. She has resolved not work with them again either.

(This is also a very good example of an Unreasonable Imposition Grudge. Many grudges can sit equally comfortably in more than one Grudge Category.)

11) INGRATITUDE GRUDGE

When someone is ungrateful or not sufficiently grateful. There's a brilliant episode in Season 9 of *Curb Your Enthusiasm*, in which Larry David is outraged that some strangers he's kindly allowed to stay in his house have only thanked him in a cursory, lukewarm way when he believes that more fulsome and enthusiastic gratitude would be appropriate. *Curb Your Enthusiasm* (like *Seinfeld* before it, the show that made David famous) is all about grudges – how we hold them and cause others to hold them with our own bad behaviour. I strongly recommend both to anyone interested in the practice of grudge-holding.

Examples
Frank always works an hour's overtime every day. One day, his boss told him off for being five minutes late back from lunch. Over fourteen years later, Frank still cannot forgive this.

Chloe's parents bought a house for her and her girlfriend Shirley to live in, rent-free. The couple lived there for years, and were saved a great deal of rent. During this period, Chloe and Shirley regularly went out for dinner with Shirley's parents, who insisted on dividing up the bill meticulously every time, and never once bought Chloe a meal, even though Chloe's parents were providing rent-free accommodation for their daughter.

12) INVALIDATION GRUDGE

When someone attacks, undermines or incorrectly counter-defines what you know from your own experience to be true.

Example
For more than twenty years, Lara was in an abusive relationship with Paul. He only hit her once – hard across the face – but he was always controlling, terrifying, bullying and emotionally manipulative. As a result, for many years he convinced Lara that she must be the one at fault, and she spent a lot of time crying and apologising. She is, happily, no longer in that relationship.

A couple of years ago, Lara was talking to a close family member, Tim, who had witnessed the abusive relationship at close range, and she said, 'Can I ask you something? When you think back to the past, to that time in our lives . . . do you have a memory of me always crying? Because in my memory, I'm always crying and apologising and begging to be forgiven during those years, but I also think that I can't have been doing that *all* the time – or else I'd have found it intolerable, and I didn't. I thought it was fine and normal while it was going on – just a normal relationship with some bad moments, like all relationships.'

Tim nodded and said, quite casually, 'Well, yes, I remember you crying a fair bit. You probably felt guilty.' He didn't seem to think that his saying this would upset Lara or strike a jarring note at all. He fully accepted her abuser's version of events: that whenever he had screamed at her, bullied her or ignored her, it was because she had done something to deserve it. It's true that she developed a habit of lying to her abuser in order to secure rare pockets of freedom and privacy for herself, but she was horrified to realise that Tim could have witnessed the way she was treated and not understand, even decades later, that she was the victim of psychological and emotional abuse and manipulation.

That Tim could think about that part of Lara's life and conclude that she was the one who needed to feel guilty is a black mark against Tim in Lara's heart for ever. The word 'guilty' hit her as hard as if he'd stamped on her life story with a heavy boot.

13) BOUNDARY VIOLATION GRUDGE

Crucially, this isn't the same as an Unreasonable Imposition Grudge. Sometimes, when people try to impose upon us, we imagine they're violating our boundaries – but if we could stop them by saying, 'No, you may not do that', and they would then listen to us, then it's not a boundary violation. A boundary violation is when you've set, or there exists, a clear boundary already and someone steps over it.

Example

As luck would have it, I suffered a spectacular boundary violation only a few days ago. I arrived at my holiday home, intending to finish an urgent writing project in peace, and was shocked to find that employees of a local holiday lettings company had let themselves into my house and changed things around without my permission.

I had agreed with this company that they would at some point come in to take an inventory of the house, with a view to me possibly letting out the place to others in the future. To this end, I had given them the code for the house's key safe. But I had no idea that they would do anything but the inventory. That was the only thing I had authorised them to do. I hadn't decided I definitely wanted to let out my house and I hadn't signed their contract.

To my horror, I discovered that they had swapped my own bedding, towels and bathmats for theirs, they'd put their company's branded toiletries in all the house's bathrooms, and many of my possessions had been hidden away in cupboards and drawers. The lettings company's branded key-ring had been attached to my key in the key safe, and my address had been written in black pen on the labels of all of my duvets. Instead of the work I needed to do, I had to spend hours riffling through the house to find the simplest things and putting everything back where and how it needed to be.

I wrote them a letter detailing all my grievances. I tried to sound as if I was furious, though in fact, my anger was diluted considerably by the thought: 'Ooh – this will make a brilliant grudge!' Once you become a practised grudge-keeper like me, dear reader, you too will be able to dilute and calm your anger simply by focusing on the great grudge potential of the incident. It is a huge relief to be able to do so, I promise you.

14) ATTEMPTED DEPRIVATION OF AGENCY GRUDGE

When someone tries to stop you making the choices and decisions that are rightfully yours to make.

Example
Soon after Luke, his wife and four-year-old daughter moved into their new home, his parents came round for lunch and, naturally, Luke and his wife gave them the full tour of the property. When they got to their daughter's bedroom, Luke's mother took one look at the bed and said, 'That's not big enough for her. You need to get her a bigger one.' Luke explained that they would obviously get their daughter a bigger bed at some point, but that for the time being, this bed was fine. Luke and his wife knew this because their daughter slept comfortably in the bed every night. She never rolled out, and there was plenty of mattress space on either side of her when she lay down.

His mother immediately became furious. 'Why can't you just do it now?' she snapped. 'You're going to do it eventually, so why not now? This bed is *not* big enough for her. It's just plain *not big enough*!'

Calmly, Luke told her that it was, and that it was his wife's and his decision, since this was their house and their daughter. Luke's mother would not accept this, and her black mood ruined the whole lunch and afternoon. She sulked, wouldn't speak to Luke and shot hostile looks at him across the lunch table. She clearly hoped he would want to cheer her up by doing what she asked, which was how he had responded to her hostile sulks for most of his childhood, but on this occasion he was determined not to give in. When his mother saw that he was showing no signs of capitulating to her bullying, she finally said, 'Look, maybe you don't think she needs a bigger bed right now . . . but couldn't you just get her one to please me? Would it really kill you to do *one* thing you don't think you need to do, just because it would please your mum?'

Luke explained to her that he was happy to try to please her in any way he considered reasonable, but that being emotionally blackmailed into replacing items of furniture in his house that he knew didn't need replacing was something he wasn't willing to allow. After hearing this answer, Luke's mother sulked and withheld affection for the rest of the visit.

15) THREAT GRUDGE

When someone threatens you in an unacceptable way. (Yes, there are acceptable ways, e.g.: 'If you don't stop kicking your sister, you're not going to get a cake for pudding.')

Example
Anne was on a bus when her best friend's husband, Greg, appeared and sat down beside her. Anne started to make small talk, but then realised that Greg was upset and in no fit state to chat. She asked him if he was okay, and he proceeded to tell her a long and involved story about a woman

at work, Cassie, who had just rejected him. He told her he'd been in love with Cassie for more than a year, would happily have left his wife Donna (Anne's best friend) for her, but she'd just rejected him, told him she'd never fancied him and that he must have got the wrong end of the stick.

Anne couldn't believe Greg was telling her all of this, knowing that she was Donna's best friend. Once he'd finished telling her his tale of woe, he clearly realised that he'd compromised security in a big way by confiding all this to someone much closer to his wife than to him. So he adopted a fake-cheerful tone, guffawed awkwardly and said, 'By the way, you'd better not tell Donna, because, ha ha!, I *would* shoot your children dead.' Anne is almost sure he was joking – but not entirely sure.

16) SELFIE GRUDGE

One of the most powerful grudge types – the grudge you hold against yourself. It's important to note, however, that Selfie grudges should not be any more powerful than other kinds of grudges purely because of their self-directedness. If we don't forgive ourselves as readily as we forgive others, and ditch Selfie grudges as easily as we ditch other-people-focused grudges, then we might be guilty of a certain amount of cowardice and self-victimisation. Too afraid to enter into any sort of conflictual relationship with a more threatening 'other', even in the privacy of our own minds, we take the easy route of berating ourselves mercilessly, having first tacitly agreed to be our own victims. This is not good, people. Be your own willing victim and you'll soon find you're playing that role for other people too. If you treat yourself fairly, you're more likely to receive fair treatment from others.

Example

Grace was involved in a friendship that had initially threatened to turn into a romance. She had been out with Angus a few times, and they had kissed once, but then things had fizzled out and they'd agreed to be friends and nothing more. Things had been further complicated by Grace being in a committed relationship (with a man called Jack) at the time. So she and Angus decided to end things before it turned into an affair.

Angus worked with Grace's brother Dave at a local engineering firm, which was how she'd met him. One evening, Grace and Jack were round at Dave and his wife's house for dinner, and Dave suddenly said to Grace, 'I need to talk to you privately. Let's go for a drive.' Jack and Dave's wife assumed it was a private brother–sister thing, and Grace herself had no idea what it was about.

As soon as they set off, Dave said, 'Are you having an affair with Angus?' She wasn't, and she and Angus had agreed that they had no plans for an affair, so she said, truthfully, 'No.'

'Don't lie,' said Dave. 'I *know* there's something going on. You need to tell me exactly what the situation is. Angus is my colleague. Tell me what's going on – the whole truth, immediately – or I'll go back to the house and tell your boyfriend you're having an affair with Angus.'

Grace was petrified. She knew that Dave would tell Jack if she disobeyed him, but she wasn't prepared to tell him that she'd kissed Angus or seen him a few times, both because it was none of his business and because it didn't seem safe to do so. What if he told Jack? Jack wouldn't be thrilled, even though no actual sex had taken place and it was now all over between Grace and Angus.

She thought fast and told Dave a story that wasn't the truth, but that would hopefully explain whatever he might have seen or overheard. She told him that Angus was in love with her friend Laura and had wanted advice, and that's why she'd met him a few times in secret.

Dave accepted this rather lame story (presumably because he was desperate to believe that his colleague and his sister weren't having a fling) and he and Grace returned to his house to rejoin the others.

Grace has been furious with herself ever since. She thinks she behaved like a spineless wimp, and that instead she should have said, 'Dave, I am under no obligation to share with you any details about my relationship with Angus, and if you threaten me again, or make good your threat, then I'm afraid I'm not going to be able to have you in my life.' Dave had no right whatsoever to demand that information as if he had a God-given right to it. Grace believes she should have told him so, and stood firm.

17) ABANDONMENT GRUDGE

When someone abandons you. The example below is very distressing and constitutes child abuse as well as cause to hold a grudge.

Example
When John was fourteen, he returned home from school to find the house all packed up, with his possessions left in

black bags outside the door. His entire family had moved away, leaving him behind. Seven years later, he found his mother and they rebuilt a relationship until, just eighteen months later, she disappeared again. John knows where his mother is now, but he isn't getting in touch. He doesn't intend to allow her a third attempt.

There are also less distressing incidents that can lead to an abandonment grudge. One can abandon dialogues, situations and creative projects as well as people. Last year, Shane expressed an interest in working with me on a particular project involving literature and theatre. We communicated enthusiastically for several months, and then at a certain point, I emailed him and he did not respond. He never got in touch with me again. For whatever reason, he had decided he did not wish to proceed with our project – a decision he could easily have written or emailed and told me about. Instead, he decided simply to disappear. I'm grateful to have had the chance to see how he conducts himself before getting too involved with him and his organisation. I would not consider working with him or them again.

18) INJUSTICE GRUDGE

When something unfair happens to you or someone else.

Example
A girls' high school gives out lots of prizes and awards every year. One of the most prestigious is the silver sports cup. One year this cup was awarded to Olivia, a very

talented student who had played very well in some netball matches. Everyone was rather surprised, however, because there was another student in the same year – let's call her Megan – who was the obvious shining sports star of the school. Everyone knew Megan had the talent to be a potential Olympic gold medal winner – she really was that good.

A few days after the awards ceremony, it emerged that the main sports teacher (whose job it was to choose the winner each year) *had* awarded the cup to Megan – or at least, she had tried to. The Head of Seniors, on hearing that the sports cup was to go to Megan, said to the sports teacher, 'I'd appreciate it if you would award the cup to Olivia instead.'

'No, I've awarded it to Megan,' said the sports teacher. 'She so clearly deserves it.'

'Yes, but Olivia hasn't won anything else,' said the Head of Seniors. 'If she doesn't get the sports cup, she won't get anything at all.'

The sports teacher, strongly suspecting that if she stood her ground she would be overruled in any case, gave in, and Olivia got the sports cup.

Guess what? Somehow, the Head of Seniors had not been informed that Olivia had in fact won *two* other prizes in addition to the sports cup. On the morning of the awards ceremony, she said to the sports teacher, 'Oh, sorry, I didn't know until this morning – and it's too late now. The sports cup has gone off to be engraved with Olivia's name.'

19) RUDENESS GRUDGE (A.K.A. NEGLIGENT TACTLESSNESS GRUDGE)

When someone is unacceptably rude. (There are circumstances in which rudeness can be acceptable – if you have provoked someone, or been rude to them first, for instance.)

Example
Samantha was once invited to a poetry festival, to do the Saturday-night reading, the main reading of the festival. More than 200 tickets had been sold for her event, about which the organisers were very happy. On the Saturday, the festival organiser, Clive, took all of the festival poets, partners and guests out for lunch. The subject of which poets to invite to the next year's festival came up, and Samantha suggested the famous poet Althea Clements, whose work she loved. Clive laughed ruefully and said, 'Huh! Can't afford her! Tried this year. You're only here because you're a poor man's Althea Clements.' A horrified hush immediately descended on the table, as you can imagine. Later Clive apologised to Samantha and insisted that she had to forgive him because he'd been far ruder to other people, and also because he was an unfortunate alcoholic whose wife had recently died.

20) ASSUMING THE WORST GRUDGE

When someone picks the worst possible interpretation of your actions and uses it against you.

Example

Bob's son Sam, a football fan, really wanted a particular Leeds United poster. When Bob's parents asked what Sam wanted for Christmas, Bob told them about the poster and they said that they would get it for him, which they did. He loved it, and wanted to put it up straight away, but Bob said, 'Listen, if we just Blu-tack it to the wall, it'll soon get dog-eared and torn. Why don't we frame it?'

'Good idea,' agreed Sam. And so that was the plan. Bob was ludicrously busy with work at the time, and life, and small children, so he couldn't go to the framers immediately. He put the poster safely away, planning to take it to the framers as soon as he had a free day. He did not, at that point, have many free days.

A few weeks later, Bob was at his parents' house and his father asked, 'So, how does the poster look on Sam's wall?'

'I haven't put it up yet,' said Bob. 'I've been so busy that I haven't—'

That was as far as he got. 'You *haven't put it up yet*?' bellowed his father. 'You've had that poster for *weeks*. Your mum and I devoted time and effort to finding that poster – the exact one he wanted. It takes five minutes to put up a poster. *Five minutes.*'

Bob felt misjudged. He later told his wife, 'There's no way I can now get that poster framed and put it up. It'd make me feel sick. You'll have to do it.'

As it turned out, there was no need. A few days later, Sam announced that he no longer supported Leeds United, but now supported Chelsea instead. To Bob, this felt very much like karma.

Other Common Grudge Types Include:

EXCLUSION GRUDGE – when you're left out by design.

COWARDICE GRUDGE – when someone is too scared to do the right thing, in a way that impacts you negatively.

INAPPROPRIATE WARNING GRUDGE – this is kind of a hard one to get your head around. It's when someone warns you about something that's *so* unlikely to happen that the warning is not only unnecessary but also constitutes an act of aggression in its own right.

OVERREACTION/RELATIVE HARMS GRUDGE – when someone overreacts to a degree that is more harmful or offensive than the inciting incident. When a person fails to weigh up the relative harms of the original offence and their response to it, and ends up causing greater and/or unnecessary damage.

UNFAIR GRUDGE GRUDGE – when you hold a grudge about someone else holding a grudge that you think they've got no right to hold.

MISUNDERSTANDING OF LOYALTY GRUDGE – when someone mistakenly believes that if you're truly loyal to them, you ought to be willing to disown/punch/slander anyone they happen not to like.

RAGE-DUMPING OR MISERY-DUMPING GRUDGE – when someone is angry or unhappy, fails to realise that this doesn't give them the right to make you unhappy too, fails to take responsibility for their own feelings and sprays their rage or misery all over you.

LIGHT-MAKING CONFESSION GRUDGE – when someone confesses to a serious past violation as if it's a trivial amusing thing, eg: 'Of course, haha, you know I used to put little bits of minced beef into your vegetarian casseroles when you weren't looking.'

APOLOGY COASTING GRUDGE – when someone uses apologies like 'Get out of jail free' cards.

There are many, many more grudge types besides these ones – please do draw any interesting ones you think of to my attention!

And now, since we've come to the end of the chapter, it's time for another of my personal grudge stories. This one is a 2-carat grudge . . .

The Famous Author
Grudge type: no 5, Hypocrisy Grudge

When I'm not writing about grudges, I'm still basically writing about grudges – by which I mean, I write crime novels. A grudge is the motive for many a fictional murder; perhaps that's why crime fiction is my favourite genre.

One of the strands of my life as a crime writer is this: at the request of Agatha Christie's family, I write continuation novels for the Agatha Christie estate, featuring

Christie's world-famous Belgian detective Hercule Poirot.

In September 2013, my new Poirot novel was announced. As it would be the first to be written since Agatha Christie's death, it was a news story all over the world. At the same time, a famous British author – let's call him Michael Baker – had a new book out, and was doing lots of publicity for it. I had heard of Michael Baker, because he's very famous, but didn't know anything about his new book.

The publishers of my forthcoming Poirot novel, HarperCollins, were sending me all mentions of it from the press, both British and international. Most of the stories were different versions of the same story: a new Hercule Poirot novel after nearly forty years! Then I came across an article from a newspaper that I imagined at first must have got mixed up with my batch by mistake: an interview with Michael Baker about his new book, published the same day that my Poirot novel news broke.

I had a quick look and saw the word 'Poirot' near the bottom of the page. Most of the questions Baker had been asked were about his book, but the last one was: 'Have you heard that there's going to be a new Hercule Poirot novel written by Sophie Hannah, at the Christie estate's request? What do you think about that?' Or words to that effect.

Baker's answer didn't surprise me at all. He said, 'Oh, is there? That strikes me as a rather second-rate thing to do. Why can't people write something original?' Many people think continuation novels are unoriginal or lazy, and so I was used to hearing that view. It's one I disagree with. Usually, every element of a continuation novel is completely original apart from the one given element – in my case, Poirot. And in non-continuation novels there are given elements too: the sky, the sun, oxygen.

This, however, is not the point. I didn't mind at all that Michael Baker didn't like the idea of a Poirot continuation novel. Other people did, though. My email in-box soon started to fill up with messages with subject headings like 'Bloody cheek!' and 'Michael Baker, f***ing hypocrite!'

I was confused. Why a hypocrite? Had Baker written a Poirot novel too, and then denied it? A Miss Marple novel, perhaps? No, I was pretty sure that was impossible. I'd have heard about it if he had, being an avid Agatha fan.

I started to open the messages and soon saw what the issue was. More than twenty people had written to tell me: Baker's new book – for which he was doing all this publicity – was a retelling of a selection of someone else's stories.

Wait – what? A *retelling*? Of stories – lots of them – that were all, without exception, made up by *somebody else*? A *retelling*?

I thought that this simply couldn't be true. No one who had just published a retelling of stories that were *completely and entirely not made up by him,* and first written by another writer, could have described a continuation novel as unoriginal and a second-rate thing to do, in public, without realising that he himself was, at that very moment, publicising something much less original. Surely not.

I hurried to the Amazon website to see how more than twenty people could possibly have made a mistake. They hadn't.

(Sorry about that stark, shocking ending, folks. There's no twist, I'm afraid – no postscript that makes it all okay. Michael Baker did not, as far as I know, jolt awake in the middle of the night soon afterwards and think, 'Oh, no! I've been a massive hypocrite! I'm going to put this right if it's the last thing I do.' I doubt that will ever happen. What's more likely to happen is that Michael Baker will publish a book about grudges one day and, when interviewed about it, he'll be asked what he thinks about *this* book, and he'll say, 'Oh, a book about grudges? How unoriginal! What a third-rate thing to do!')

So, I've given you a 1-carat grudge (*The Taxi That Didn't Move*) and now a 2-carat grudge. I'm certain some of you are starting to wonder: what, in the name of all things grudge-worthy, does all this carat terminology and classification mean? Read on to find out!

4

How to Grade a Grudge

'You see, I am not malicious, or I could easily insert here the name of some twaddler against whom I have a grudgekin.'

Anthony Trollope

Now that we've looked at some key grudge types, we're going to move on to the next important question: once you've got your grudge and identified its theme, how do you assess it for grudgeworthiness? Is it a vital, powerful (bigger) grudge or a relatively frivolous, trivial (smaller) one? And how can we accurately assess the size and power of a grudge when grudges are not real, physical objects?

No one has ever invented a grudge-grading system, so, once again, I decided to give it a go. Once again, also, I consulted my husband. 'There are two things you'd need to consider, for each grudge,' he said.

'Only two?' This sounded wrong to me.

'Yeah. The "Grrrr" factor, and how long you've held the grudge.'

I had, in fact, already done some work on a grudge-grading system, which I really liked and which was markedly different from the one my husband was suggesting. Since we were the only two people on the planet (as far as I know) who had ever given any thought to the matter of how to grade and measure a grudge, I decided that if I added his measurable factors to my measurable factors, we would end up with a foolproof system:

The Carat-based Grudge Grading System

Carats, as you might already know, are used to measure the weight of diamonds. Like diamonds, grudges can be on the lighter or weightier side (and, of course, they can and should sparkle, both in our grudge cabinets and in our minds!) so I've decided to use a carat-based grading system.

Here's how to grade a grudge. Call your grudge to mind and answer the following questions about it:

1. Was the intention of the grudgee:

a) definitely or probably bad

b) possibly bad

c) not bad

2. Did they know they were upsetting or hurting you?

a) Yes, definitely

b) Possibly

c) Not at all

3. Was the overall situation:

a) very serious

b) quite serious

c) not very serious

4. Was the effect upon you of what they did or said:

a) very bad

b) quite bad

c) not so bad

5. Should or could they have known/done better?

a) Yes

b) Maybe

c) No

6. Did they cause you real harm?

a) Yes

b) Maybe

c) No

7. Is the 'Grrrr!' factor (the extent to which you still strongly feel 'Wow, that was *so* out of order!' when you think about the incident now) of this grudge:

a) high

b) medium

c) low

8. Have you held this grudge:

a) for ages; or, for not very long but you know it'll last for ever?

b) for a medium length of time; or, for a short time and you think you'll hold it for a bit longer but not for ever?

c) for a short time, and you'll probably have given up this grudge by next week?

For each of your answers to the above questions, award your grudge 3 points for an a) answer, 2 for a b) answer and 1 for a c) answer. You'll then have a total number of points. Take this number forward to the next part of the grading process:

9. Would this incident, alone, be sufficient to make you hold a grudge about this person or people?

a) Yes

b) No, only with other incidents taken into account too

If you answered a), your total points remain unchanged. If you answered b), deduct 1 point from your total.

10. Would something bad or frightening have happened to your grudgee if they *hadn't* performed the grudge-sparking action?

a) No

b) Yes

If you answered a), your total points remain unchanged. If you answered b), deduct 1 point from your total.

11. Would this grudge be cancelled out/terminated if your grudgee apologised fully and wholeheartedly?

a) No

b) Yes

If you answered a), your total points remain unchanged. If you answered b), deduct 1 point from your total.

12. Is your grudgee someone who matters to you, and to whom you matter?

a) Yes, massively

b) Yes, quite a lot

c) Not especially – only as a fellow human being

If you answered a), add 4 points. If you answered b), add 2 points. If c), leave your score as it is.

Well done! Your grudge now has a total number of points. Now for the grading:

13 points or fewer = a 1-carat grudge
14 points = a 2-carat grudge
15 points = a 3-carat grudge
16 points = a 4-carat grudge
17 points = a 5-carat grudge
18 points = a 6-carat grudge
19 points = a 7-carat grudge
20 points = an 8-carat grudge
21 points = a 9-carat grudge
22 or above = a 10-carat grudge

A 10-carat grudge is the strongest, weightiest, most powerful kind of grudge a person can hold, and a 1-carat grudge is the lightest and least significant. Ideally, your Grudge Cabinet should have a good mix of all the different carats.

Let's look again at the examples of my 1- and 2-carat grudges, *The Taxi That Didn't Move* and *The Famous Author,* to see how this grudge-grading system works in practice. My answers are in **bold**.

GRADING *THE TAXI THAT DIDN'T MOVE* GRUDGE:

1. Was the intention of the grudgee (Vern):

a) definitely or probably bad

b) possibly bad

c) not bad – Vern is neurotic, but his only aim was to check everyone was safe. (1 point)

2. Did they know they were upsetting or hurting you?

a) Yes, definitely

b) Possibly

c) Not at all – it wouldn't have crossed his mind that his neurosis might have had any negative effect upon me. (1 point)

3. Was the overall situation:

a) very serious

b) quite serious

c) **not very serious – no one was ever in danger and nothing much was at stake. (1 point)**

4. Was the effect upon you of what they did or said:

a) very bad

b) quite bad

c) **not so bad – I was briefly shaken and angry, but soon got over it and thought it was funny. (1 point)**

5. Should or could they have known/done better?

a) Yes

b) **Maybe – on the one hand, yes, Vern totally should have known better than to be so silly. On the other hand, he was incapable of knowing better because of his neurosis, which was severe enough to qualify as a condition. (2 points)**

c) No

6. Did they cause you real harm?

a) Yes

b) Maybe

c) No (1 point)

7. Is the 'Grrrr!' factor of this grudge:

a) high

b) medium

**c) low – my main feeling is not 'Grrrr' but 'What a
shame for Vern that he's so neurotic'. (1 point)**

8. Have you held this grudge:

**a) for ages – since 2007. I will always want to
remember that Vern did this, and limit his ability,
and that of others, to inflict their neuroses on me
in future. (3 points)**

b) for a medium length of time; or, for a short time and
you think you'll hold it for a bit longer but not for ever.

c) for a short time, and you'll probably have given up this
grudge by next week.

My *Taxi That Didn't Move* grudge has 11 points so far.

Take this number forward to the next part of the grading process:

9. Would this incident, alone, be sufficient to make you hold
a grudge about this person or people?

a) Yes – so no points are deducted

b) No, only with other incidents taken into account too

10. Would something bad or frightening have happened to your grudgee if they *hadn't* performed the grudge-sparking action?

a) No

b) Yes – Vern, in his neurotic panic, was convinced that if he didn't watch me until I walked back into my house, something horrendous might have happened to my children. So he would have felt uneasy and worried all the way home. (Minus 1 point)

11. Would this grudge be cancelled out/terminated if your grudgee apologised fully and wholeheartedly?

a) No

b) Yes – if Vern had some therapy and one day said, 'I was totally in the grip of irrational paranoia in those days, I'm so sorry if that adversely affected you,' then the grudge would be cancelled out. (Minus 1 point)

12. Is your grudgee someone who matters to you, and to whom you matter?

a) Yes, massively (4 points added)

b) Yes, quite a lot

c) Not especially

So we end up with a total of 13 points for *The Taxi That Didn't Move,* making it a 1-carat grudge. And, since we've also looked at grudge types in this chapter, there are many that could work for this particular grudge story: Inappropriate Warning Grudge is probably the one I'd choose, but it might also be Neurosis-Dumping Grudge (a variation of the Rage-Dumping or Misery-Dumping Grudge), or an Overreaction Grudge.

GRADING *THE FAMOUS AUTHOR* GRUDGE:

1. Was the intention of the grudgee **(Michael Baker)**:

a) definitely or probably bad

b) possibly bad

c) **not bad – I'm certain the hypocrisy involved won't have crossed his mind. I don't think he thought about his own book at all when he was asked about my Poirot continuation novel. My guess is that he has a unquestioned core belief that they reside in different leagues of literary worthiness, and so it simply wouldn't occur to him to think of the two together, even when doing so would enable him to avoid massive hypocrisy. (1 point)**

2. Did they know they were upsetting, hurting **or being unfair to** you?

a) Yes, definitely

b) Possibly

c) Not at all (1 point)

3. Was the overall situation:

a) very serious

b) quite serious

c) not very serious (1 point)

4. Was the effect upon you of what they did or said:

a) very bad

b) quite bad

c) not so bad (1 point)

5. Should or could they have known/done better?

a) Yes – definitely. He's a very clever man and it ought to have been obvious to him that he was being a big hypocrite. (3 points)

b) Maybe

c) No

6. Did they cause you real harm?

a) Yes

b) Maybe

c) No (1 point)

7. Is the 'Grrrr!' factor of this grudge:

a) high – I still feel a huge Grrrr about it. To casually call someone's book unoriginal and second-rate before it's even been written, when you've taken unoriginality several steps further yourself, is deserving of all the Grrrrs. (3 points)

b) medium

c) low

8. Have you held this grudge:

a) for ages – since 2013 (3 points)

b) for a medium length of time; or, for a short time and you think you'll hold it for a bit longer but not for ever.

c) for a short time, and you'll probably have given up this grudge by next week.

My *The Famous Author* grudge has 14 points so far.

9. Would this incident, alone, be sufficient to make you hold a grudge about this person or people?

a) Yes – so no points are deducted.

b) No, only with other incidents taken into account too.

10. Would something bad or frightening have happened to your grudgee if they *hadn't* performed the grudge-sparking action?

a) No – so no points are deducted.

b) Yes

11. Would this grudge be cancelled out/terminated if your grudgee apologised fully and wholeheartedly?

a) No – so no points are deducted. I've already forgiven him, and I'd appreciate the apology, but the knowledge that an intelligent person could be so hypocritical and not even realise it would always be something I'd want to remember – to make sure I'm never that hypocritical myself. It's too easy to assume that your actions are innately superior to other people's, but anyone who doesn't question that constantly is likely to end up behaving suboptimally.

b) Yes

12. Is your grudgee someone who matters to you, and to whom you matter?

a) Yes, massively

b) Yes, quite a lot

c) Not especially – only as a fellow human being (so points stay the same)

My *The Famous Author* grudge ends up with a total of 14 points, making it a 2-carat grudge.

And now it's time for one of my 3-carat grudges:

The Painting in a Haystack
Grudge type: no. 2, Unreasonable Imposition Grudge

This is not a story about a painting that was actually in a haystack, as the title might suggest; I'd moved a few days earlier, and I still had lots of taped-up boxes full of stuff piled up in corners in the rooms of my new house. Trying to find any individual item would have been like looking for the proverbial needle in a haystack.

At the time, I had two children aged two and three, and was writing my third crime novel, and travelling around all over the place promoting my first and second crime novels, and meanwhile my husband was working full-time and getting back from work quite late, so I was busy. As busy as I've ever been, probably.

Since we'd moved, I had unpacked only the boxes labelled 'Open first'. Any box that wasn't labelled in a way that indicated urgency was waiting until I had a spare two or three days to finish unpacking properly.

My brother Ted and his wife Laura were desperate to come round as soon as possible to see the new house. 'Great!' I said, looking forward to showing them round. Laura is a painter. She's also a sensitive, volatile person. When she takes something personally, or when something doesn't go the way she hopes it will, she takes her bad moods out on Ted. I've seen this happen many times and I can attest that, on these occasions, Ted's suffering is not insignificant. Much as I love Laura, I would rather be single for ever than married to someone like her. She's stuck in a state of emotional childhood, after having had a chaotic and traumatic actual childhood.

My husband and I often used to speculate about why Ted stays with Laura, since neither of us could possibly stay in a relationship like that, and we've agreed that it's likely that Ted can't bear the thought of being alone; and he would fear that, if he found someone new, they might be as difficult as Laura or even worse.

A few years before we moved house, Laura had given me a present: one of her paintings – a small oil painting of four women standing in the middle of a road with their arms outstretched, as if they were about to take off and fly. I loved it. In the house we'd just sold, it had been on the lounge wall, so I'd packed it in one of several boxes marked 'Lounge', so that it could go up on the new lounge wall.

On the day that Ted and Laura were due to come round for dinner and a full house tour, I was in London for a series of meetings with my agent and my publishers. Between meetings, I saw I had a message from Ted. It read:

> Just had a quick thought: Laura's painting that she gave you – have you put it up yet?

I replied:

> No, not yet. Only urgent stuff unpacked so far! xxx

Ted responded:

> Sorry to be a pain, but is there any way you could put it up before we get there tonight? If we come and it's not up, Laura will be upset.

I texted back:

> Soz, just not possible. I'm in meetings all day, then on train back, then have to drive to childminder to get kids. I don't know which box it's in – and don't have time to look! xxx

Ted said:

> Won't the box it's in be marked 'Pictures/paintings'? Please, if you could possibly find it, it'll make my life MUCH easier. And it won't just be me that gets it in the neck if the painting's not on the wall – she'll hold it

against you too. Would really advise you find painting and put it up. Thanks and sorry for the hassle. V much looking forward to seeing house.

A strange, hot, prickly feeling started to spread across my skin, all over my body. I rang Ted before I could chicken out of doing what I was, in that moment, angry enough to want to do.

'Can I ask you something?' I said when he answered. 'Instead of pestering me to do something that I've told you I don't have time to do today, and that I shouldn't *have* to do today, why don't you go and pester Laura? Why don't you text her and say, "Hey Laura, if we go round to Sophie's new house tonight and she hasn't yet put your painting up because most of her possessions are still in boxes, I don't want you to give me or her a hard time about that – okay?"'

'I can't say that to her,' Ted told me.

'Why not?' I asked. 'You could say, "Look, you know Sophie loves that painting. She's just been too busy to unpack, and that's the only reason it's still in a box. Don't take it personally or get upset about it, because that would be daft." Or, if you're too scared to say that to her, I could say it!'

'No, please don't say anything,' said Ted nervously.

'All right, I won't,' I said. 'But, in future, please don't try to emotionally blackmail me into doing something you have no right to pressure me into doing, just because you're too scared to confront the person whose attitude and behaviour needs to change. Don't threaten me with Laura's anger or disappointment, either. If you're going to put effort into trying to resolve a potential problem, direct your efforts towards the person who would be the unreasonable cause of the potential trouble – Laura, in other words. Not me. If you want to be emotionally blackmailed by her, that's up to you, but don't try to pass it on to me.'

'Yes, you're right, I'm sorry,' said Ted, who had been saying some variation of those words regularly for many years. I could hear how easy it was for him to add me to his mental list of people he said them to. 'It won't happen again,' he muttered, full of contrition. (I knew it would, and it did. By this point, Ted's responses to Laura's behaviour were hard-wired into his brain. He would never be able to stand up to her, or even to suggest that she approach something from a different angle.)

I remember thinking to myself, 'I wish I could cancel Ted and Laura's visit this evening.' Technically I could have, of course, but I was as much of a coward as Ted. Most of us are cowards when it comes to dealing with the people we're afraid of. I wasn't nearly as afraid of Laura as Ted was, but I wasn't entirely unafraid of her either. I knew she had the power to ruin my evening and next few days if she chose to – and she had chosen to do so many times in the years I'd known her.

I attended two more meetings, then caught the train home, collected my children, went home and cooked dinner so that it would be ready for Ted and Laura. Half an hour before they arrived, hating myself as I did it, I opened at random one of the boxes with 'Lounge' written on it. If the painting wasn't in there, which it almost definitely wouldn't be, there was no way I was going to open any more—

Oh. There was the painting, staring up at me.

I had no idea which box contained the picture hooks, but the house's previous owners had left some in the wall, so I hung Laura's painting on one of those. In due course she and Ted arrived, she approved of where I'd hung it and the evening went smoothly. Everyone seemed to be having fun (including me, even though I actually wasn't). At the end of the night, Ted mouthed, 'Thank you' at me, which made me want to scream. I hadn't put the picture up for his sake, because he'd asked me to. I'd put it up because it happened to be in the first box I opened, and because I didn't want our evening to be dominated by Laura sulkily chewing her bottom lip. I didn't want Ted's thanks. It felt like a slap in the face. I shrugged at him as if to say, 'No idea what you mean, mate.'

I felt that by thanking me, Ted was effectively cancelling out his earlier apology. He now seemed to think it was fine that he'd tried to scare me into putting up Laura's picture, and that I'd ended up doing so. It was an 'all's well that ends well' kind of thank you. If his apology was genuine, why didn't he mouth 'sorry' or 'you shouldn't have'?

I haven't got this grudge about Ted because he asked to do a time-consuming thing that I had no time or energy to do. If he'd pressured me to go on a three-day hike with him, I'd have explained that I didn't have time and asked not to be pestered about it, but there would have been no grudge. What made me want to bookmark the incident in my mind, and what still gives *The Painting in a Haystack* a live charge of relevance, is the knowledge that in certain situations, Ted would rather put unfair pressure on me, even knowing I was overwhelmed and overloaded both practically and emotionally, than tell an entirely unreasonable narcissist that he's not going to act as a conduit for her emotional blackmail of his sister.

I took the picture off the wall as soon as Ted and Laura had left. In less than twenty-four hours, I had gone from loving it to loathing it. Since that day, it has never been up on my wall – apart from when I've known Laura was coming round.

Some years later, Laura exited Ted's life, and mine too. (I wish I could say he dumped her, but that wasn't how it happened.) As soon as I knew Laura was never likely to come to my house again, I gave the painting away to a local charity shop.

GRADING *THE PAINTING IN A HAYSTACK* GRUDGE:

1. Was the intention of the grudgee **(Ted)**:

a) definitely or probably bad

b) possibly bad

c) **not bad – he just wanted to avoid trouble for all of us. (1 point)**

2. Did they know they were upsetting, hurting **or being unfair to** you?

a) Yes, definitely

b) Possibly

c) **Not at all – not until I pointed it out. (1 point)**

3. Was the overall situation:

a) very serious

b) quite serious

c) not very serious (1 point)

4. Was the effect upon you of what they did or said:

a) very bad

b) quite bad – when I had very young children and my husband was still working full-time, I was more stressed than I've ever been. Ted colluded with a wholly unreasonable person to put more pressure on me at that time, which told me that my well-being doesn't matter all that much to my brother. Knowing he had that thought – 'It's easier to bully Sophie than to have Laura bully me' – permanently affected the degree to which I feel I can trust and rely on him. (2 points)

c) not so bad

5. Should or could they have known/done better?

a) Yes

b) Maybe

c) No – Ted should have known better, but he simply couldn't have done better because his fear of Laura's wrath was so debilitating to him. (1 point)

6. Did they cause you real harm?

a) Yes

b) Maybe

c) No (1 point)

7. Is the 'Grrrr!' factor of this grudge:

a) high – I love Ted to bits, but I still get all the Grrrrs when I think about this – probably because it wasn't the only occasion on which he asked me if I could make my own situation a bit worse in order to placate Laura. (3 points)

b) medium

c) low

8. Have you held this grudge:

a) for ages – since 2007 (3 points)

b) for a medium length of time; or, for a short time and you think you'll hold it for a bit longer but not for ever.

c) for a short time, and you'll probably have given up this
  grudge by next week.

My *The Painting in a Haystack* grudge has 13 points so
far.

9. Would this incident, alone, be sufficient to make you hold
a grudge about this person or people?

a) Yes – so no points are deducted.

b) No, only with other incidents taken into account too.

10. Would something bad or frightening have happened to
your grudgee if they *hadn't* performed the grudge-sparking
action?

a) No – so no points are deducted.

**b) Yes – Ted was properly scared of what would
  happen if he and Laura came to my house and
  that painting was not yet up on the wall. (minus 1
  point)**

11. Would this grudge be cancelled out/terminated if your
grudgee apologised fully and wholeheartedly?

a) No

**b) Yes – since Laura exited his life, Ted has avoided
  all romantic relationships. This is sad for him,**

and it's partly because he associates romantic relationships with lack of freedom, but I strongly suspect that it's also partly because he doesn't ever again want to be in a position where he's so scared of someone that he'll end up excusing or colluding with their terrible behaviour. I think Ted genuinely regrets the way his fear made him behave while he and Laura were married. (minus 1 point)

12. Is your grudgee someone who matters to you, and to whom you matter?

a) Yes, massively (4 points)

b) Yes, quite a lot

c) Not especially

The Painting in a Haystack grudge ends up with a total of 15 points, making it a 3-carat grudge.

5

Grudge Is All Around Us

'The Bible tells us to love our neighbours and also to love our enemies; probably because generally they are the same people.'

G. K. Chesterton

When I was considering writing this book, a friend asked me, 'Do you think it's a bit of a niche subject? I mean, most people probably don't talk or think about grudges in the way we do. Maybe you shouldn't have "grudge" in the book's title.'

'Really?' I said. 'But that's the opposite of what people always say: your book's title should reflect, as clearly as possible, what it's about. And my book is *all* about grudges.'

'Yes, but I just wonder if most people, seeing the word "grudge", might not relate to it. It might not be a word they use much, or part of their everyday vocabulary.'

I don't know if my friend was right or not (she was in favour of calling this book *You're Dead to Me* instead of *How to Hold a Grudge* because she said that *was* a phrase everyone would recognise and relate to), but I *do* know that grudges are not something that only I hold.

Many of us might not talk or think about grudges every day, but that doesn't mean they aren't everywhere you look. Politics is brimming with them: Gordon Brown's grudge against Tony Blair over who ought to be Prime Minister; Jimmy Carter's grudge against Ted Kennedy for his failure (as Carter saw it) to get healthcare legislation passed during his administration. The Clintons are rumoured to have kept a 'for me and against me' database. This is not something I would advise you to do, dear reader. It's a very different practice from maintaining a balanced and enlightening Grudge Cabinet full of stories you've learned valuable lessons from. An article by Tracy Moore in *MEL* magazine says:

> *Psychologists say people who hold grudges are people who do something called 'splitting', which involves seeing the world and the people in it as either all good or all bad – with no gray zone in between. If you've ever heard someone use a phrase like, 'You're either for me or against me,' then you've got a classic splitter, and probably a grudge-holder, on your hands.*

This sort of splitting can also be a sign of narcissistic personality disorder and can lead to you holding lots of invalid Disloyalty Grudges, and to your grudgees holding valid Misunderstanding of Loyalty Grudges about you. Later in this book you will find a grudge story, *The Bellowing in the Kitchen*, which neatly illustrates the dangers of the splitter mindset.

History and popular culture are full of grudges. Here are some examples:

Bette Davis and Joan Crawford. These two Hollywood giants did their best to work together harmoniously, but it was an open secret that they hated one another. There were many petty attacks and counter-attacks. On the set of the film *What Ever Happened to Baby Jane?*, Davis installed a Coca-Cola vending machine, because Crawford's late husband had been the CEO of Pepsi. In a scene where Davis had to drag Crawford across the floor, Crawford filled her pockets with stones to make herself as heavy as possible. When Davis and not Crawford was nominated for an Oscar, Crawford talked the other nominees into letting her accept the award on their behalf. A recent TV drama about the pair showed Davis reacting to news of Crawford's death with the words, 'You should never say bad things about the dead, only good. Joan Crawford is dead? Good.'

Olivia de Havilland, another Hollywood actress, bore a grudge against her sister Joan Fontaine. In 1937, the two sisters were nominated for the same Oscar. Fontaine won, and this led to a decades-long estrangement. Fontaine once said, 'Olivia has always said I was first at everything. I got married first, got an Academy Award first, had a child first. If I die, she'll be furious, because again I'll have got there first'.

Novelists **Salman Rushdie and John le Carré** had a literary feud that started when le Carré criticised *The Satanic Verses* for mocking religious values. The two men seem to have held grudges about one another for some years, until they partially resolved the matter. (Neither writer has completely apologised, but they have both said nice things about each other's work and, we must hope, thrown their grudges about each other out of their Grudge Cabinets.)

Madonna took umbrage when Lady Gaga used a bassline in her song 'Born This Way' that sounds like the bassline to Madonna's 'Express Yourself'. Madonna said in an interview that the new song was 'reductive . . . look it up', and on her next tour she sang a mashup of the two songs. Gaga only commented on the issue once, dismissively, and Madonna has since claimed that there is no feud between them and that the story has been exaggerated by the media. The two singers, who had previously performed together, have never appeared in the same place since.

The artist **Stuart Semple** has the most wonderful grudge – possibly my favourite in this whole book! He has a grudge against fellow artist Anish Kapoor. In 2016, a military company developed the blackest pigment of black paint that had ever been created. Kapoor struck a deal with the company, securing himself exclusive rights to this black paint and preventing other artists from using it. As revenge, Semple developed a series of unique colours and pigments, which he sells on his website to anyone in the world apart from Anish Kapoor and those connected to him. To buy Semple's paints, you must first prove you have no link to Kapoor.

Noel Gallagher, frontman of the rock band Oasis, held a grudge against his brother Liam because, aged fifteen, the latter urinated all over Noel's new stereo sound system. The brothers went on to form the band – and then break it up and stop speaking to each other altogether. They reportedly reconciled in December 2017, and Liam tweeted 'We're all good again'.

Actress **Debbie Reynolds** held a long-running, civil-on-the-surface grudge against fellow star Elizabeth Taylor. Reynolds's husband divorced her to marry Taylor. Reynolds claimed to bear no grudge, but at Taylor's funeral, she couldn't resist a quip: 'No one could equal Elizabeth's beauty and sexuality. Women liked her and men adored her – my husband included.'

Fred Astaire and Ginger Rogers, famous dancing partners, came to blows on the set of *Top Hat* (1935). Dancing in the number 'Cheek to Cheek', Rogers wore a feathery dress and the ostrich feathers came loose and made a huge mess. Astaire had a tantrum about this and thereafter referred to Rogers as 'Feathers'. The two dancers continued to play romantic partners in several films, but it is said that off-stage they hardly spoke.

Taylor Swift sings about and publicises her grudges all the time. A good example is the video for the song 'Bad Blood', in which she fights and destroys a woman who resembles the singer Katy Perry. The previous year, Perry took three of Swift's backup dancers on her world tour, which is rumoured to be the origin of Swift's grudge.

V.S. Naipaul and Paul Theroux. After being great friends for many years, Theroux discovered that Naipaul had given away one of Theroux's novels, one that Theroux had personally inscribed to Naipaul and had assumed he would treasure for ever. Theroux, presumably, interpreted Naipaul's getting rid of the novel as meaning that Naipaul did not value his friendship sufficiently.

13 per cent of the USA. According to a YouGov poll from 2014, 13 per cent of Americans still feel negatively towards Great Britain as a nation 'because it tried to prevent the United States from becoming independent' in 1776.

In **Mary Shelley's novel *Frankenstein***, the monster holds a grudge against Dr Frankenstein for giving him life.

In **Emily Brontë's *Wuthering Heights***, many of the characters hold grudges that are shaped by childhood grievances and also somehow connected to property ownership in West Yorkshire.

Agatha Christie's *The Mirror Crack'd from Side to Side* features an amusing rivalry between two faded Hollywood stars. The motive for the murder is a fascinating and unusual grudge, and the way the character comes to hold the grudge is compelling and unique. (I can't reveal any more without spoilers, I'm afraid – but this is one of the great grudge-based crime novels of all time.) Christie's *Murder on the Orient Express* is another brilliant grudge-based detective novel.

There are thousands of songs about grudges, also. (I haven't added them all up, but I'm assuming there must be thousands, because a random look at the hundreds of songs I have on my phone reveals that nearly half of them are grudge-centric.) Country music has some amazing grudge-based songs, with brilliant titles like 'God May Forgive You

(But I Won't)' and 'I Hope You're Never Happy (With Anybody But Me)'. In rock and pop music, there's 'You Oughta Know' by Alanis Morissette and 'Fuck It (I Don't Want You Back)' by Eamon.

Movies are as full of grudges as songs are: *Cape Fear, Gladiator, Unforgiven, Straw Dogs, Carrie, Jaws: The Revenge, High Plains Drifter,* and many more.

I have written many poems about grudges, and so have other poets — from Catullus, a Roman poet, to the present day. Here is one of my favourite contemporary grudge poems, by the brilliant Nic Aubury:

RSVP

It seems that you like me enough that you'd ask me
To buy you a coffee machine,
Some porcelainware, a patio chair,
Or a Villeroy & Boch figurine;
Enough that you'd ask for a Waterford vase
Or a full set of white, cotton bedding,
But not quite enough that you'd actually like me
To come to the whole of your wedding.

Grudges also show up in some unexpected places where it might not occur to us to look. A recent obituary in a local American newspaper ended with the words 'She will not be missed by Gina and Jay, and they understand that this world is a better place without her.'

An article on the website mentalfloss.com revealed that both crows and ravens hold grudges. A study carried out by researchers from a Swedish university found that ravens could distinguish between 'fair' and 'unfair' interactions with humans, and held grudges against 'cheaters' for several weeks. Very sensible of them, I should say.

On 21 June 2018, the *Guardian* website published an article headlined 'Spite Buildings: When Human Grudges Get Architectural'. The case studies included: a skyscraper built specifically to block a grudgee's view of his church; one house built to block somebody's sea view, another to block out sunlight; and a house built in an alley, by someone tired of being disturbed, so that horse-drawn wagons couldn't drive noisily through the alley at night.

The advice to forgive and think positive has been around for some time in enlightened quarters. Yet it doesn't seem to be catching on. When I look at any internet discussion platform, the mood is generally much more 'I'm going to paint my house red and white to fuck with my neighbours' heads' than 'I forgive you. Let us walk, hand in harmonious hand, into our conflict-free future.' This is why the teachings of the Grudge-fold Path are so urgently needed. In a world that is full to the brim with grudges, simply telling people 'Don't have grudges' is not going to work. It's about as effective as wading into the sea while saying, 'Come on now, don't get wet.' The Grudge-fold Path (to which you will be introduced in detail in Chapter 7) says, 'We've all felt like building a spite mansion sometimes – why not draw or paint a picture of the one you'd like to build? It might look beautiful and cheer you up. You're not harming anyone.'

Who's ready for my 4-carat grudge story? It's a bit of a tearjerker, I warn you . . .

The Baby in the Heart-Shaped Frame
Grudge type: no. 20, Assuming The Worst Grudge

One of my most treasured possessions is a picture of my daughter in a tiny heart-shaped frame. It was taken on the day she was born. In our old house, it lived in my writing room, along with an equally tiny, equally treasured framed photo of my son on the day he was born. (Many years later, in a new house in a different part of the country, these two photographs would be joined by a third: our Welsh Terrier, Brewster, as a puppy. My tiny framed photo collection means a lot to me, and I don't care that some guests see it and think, 'Oh, my God, she's got a photo of the *dog* next to her two kids, as if he's an actual person!')

All of our other framed family photos were on the shelves in the dining room, but these little ones of my son and daughter were my favourites, so I took them to my writing room so that I could see them when I was working.

One day, an old friend, Heather, came to visit. I'd recently had my writing room redecorated, and Heather wanted to see it. My four-year-old daughter came too (she loved giving people tours of our house). My writing room wasn't in the main house but in an annexe – a part of the house my daughter didn't very often go to because it wasn't near either to her bedroom or to the room where she normally played. We'd never lived in a big house before and this one was massive, sprawling and old. I was finding it harder to keep on top of things than I had when we lived in a small, square, modern house in which everything was near everything else.

The first thing my daughter noticed, on entering my writing room, was the small picture of herself in a gold heart-shaped frame. 'Mummy, that's a picture of me!' she said proudly, while Heather was ooh-ing and ah-ing over the yellow silk curtains and the stripy carpet.

I told her that it was the first photo of her that anyone ever took, and she was clearly impressed and slightly awestruck by this. Heather came over to look, and said what a beautiful photo it was. 'Can I have it?' my daughter asked hopefully. 'I want to keep it. I want it to be mine.'

Since we'd moved into this new house, my children had mislaid about twenty of their favourite toys. I wasn't the only one struggling with the nooks, crannies and unexpected cupboards, it seemed. The children being both under five, they hadn't yet developed the knack of thinking back to when they last remembered having a particular item, so lots of things got lost. Some reappeared in due course; others didn't.

I knew that if I gave my daughter the photo in the heart-shaped frame, there was a good chance she'd wander off with it, get distracted, tuck it into a small gap next to a skirting board somewhere and forget all about it, and then I might never see it again. I couldn't face this prospect – most things are replaceable, but, although I had many other photos of my daughter, I knew that this particular picture, in this particular frame, had so much sentimental value to me that it was irreplaceable.

I said, 'Darling, I can't give you this photo because it's my favourite photo of you and I don't want to risk it getting lost, but I can give you another photo of you in a nice frame. Shall we go and choose one?'

My daughter's face crumpled and she started to cry. 'But I want *this* one!' she wailed. 'Why can't I have it? I want the *first* photo of me. I want it!'

Heather (whose business this discussion was none of) started to make tutting, tongue-clicking noises. I looked up to see why strange sounds were coming from my friend, and, to my immense surprise, I saw that Heather was staring at me with disgust all over her face. She shook her head as if she'd witnessed a terrible act of cruelty, tutted again and said, 'Come on! Just give it to her.'

'Yes, just give it to me!' my daughter joined in hopefully.

I said to Heather, 'I really don't want to lose it. If I let her take it off somewhere, there's a good chance I'll never see it again, and it's really important to me.' To my daughter I said, 'Hey, I can think of a photo you'll like even more – of you with Daddy, *also* taken on the day you were born.'

My daughter immediately cheered up at this prospect. Heather did not. 'That's just *mean,* Sophie,' she said. 'Why don't you just give her the photograph she really wants?'

'I've told you why,' I said. 'Because I'm scared she'll lose it, and I don't want to lose it.'

Once more, Heather's mouth contorted in disgust and she shook her head as if to say, 'I've witnessed some cold-hearted parenting in my time, but this really breaks all records of motherly awfulness.'

I was shocked, and still am, that a supposedly good friend of mine could interpret me desperately not wanting to lose a photo of my daughter as me being mean to my daughter, even after she'd heard me explain my reasons to her three times.

I thought of something else that Heather had said to me a few weeks earlier, which felt kind of connected to this incident as it related to my parenting. I had been telling Heather and another friend that a woman in her mid-sixties who had recently come to stay with me had told me she'd been impressed when I'd explained to my children that they shouldn't interrupt when grown-ups are talking. Heather immediately sneered and said aggressively, 'Yeah, I bet she was impressed that you told your kids to *shut the fuck up* so that you and she could talk instead. That's how her generation brought up their kids, to be seen and not heard.'

There was real venom in the way she said 'shut the fuck up'. Also, it wasn't accurate. I hadn't ever told my children to shut the fuck up, and Heather knew this. I *had* told my children that if we had grown-up guests, then if possible they should let the grown-ups talk and not interrupt unless it was important.

There were many, many other similar incidents – times when Heather either expressed disgust or yelled or sneered at me because of something about the way I was bringing up my children – but the photo in the heart-shaped frame is the one that hurt the most, and filled me with the most disbelief.

GRADING *THE BABY IN THE HEART-SHAPED FRAME* GRUDGE:

1. Was the intention of the grudgee **(Heather)**:

a) definitely or probably bad

**b) possibly bad – I'm going with this option
because I just don't know. Maybe Heather really**

thought I was being mean to my daughter, but
. . . it was so obvious that I wasn't! It felt to me
more as if she wanted to needle me by chipping
away at my confidence in my mothering
abilities. (2 points)

c) not bad

2. Did they know they were upsetting, hurting or being
unfair to you?

a) Yes, definitely

b) Possibly (see above) (2 points)

c) Not at all

3. Was the overall situation:

a) very serious

b) quite serious

c) not very serious (1 point)

4. Was the effect upon you of what they did or said:

a) very bad

b) quite bad

c) not so bad – after the shock wore off, I realised Heather couldn't be trusted and didn't have my best interests at heart. I took emotional precautions in all my dealings with her thereafter. (1 point)

5. Should or could they have known/done better?

a) Yes (3 points)

b) Maybe

c) No

6. Did they cause you real harm?

a) Yes

b) Maybe

c) No (1 point)

7. Is the 'Grrrr!' factor of this grudge:

a) high

b) medium – it's too sad to be full-on Grrrr. It's a medium, melancholy Grrrr. (2 points)

c) low

8. Have you held this grudge:

a) for ages – since 2006/7 (3 points)

b) for a medium length of time; or, for a short time and you think you'll hold it for a bit longer but not for ever.

c) for a short time, and you'll probably have given up this grudge by next week.

My *The Baby in the Heart-Shaped Frame* grudge has 15 points so far.

9. Would this incident, alone, be sufficient to make you hold a grudge about this person or people?

a) Yes – so no points are deducted

b) No, only with other incidents taken into account too

10. Would something bad or frightening have happened to your grudgee if they *hadn't* performed the grudge-sparking action?

a) No – so no points are deducted

b) Yes

11. Would this grudge be cancelled out/terminated if your grudgee apologised fully and wholeheartedly?

a) No

b) Yes, as long as she apologised for her slurs about my mothering skills (minus 1 point)

12. Is your grudgee someone who matters to you, and to whom you matter?

a) Yes, massively

b) Yes, quite a lot. She was an old friend, but when I was a teenager she'd been awful to me for a long period, so I was slightly wary of her even before this incident took place. (2 points)

c) Not especially

The Baby in the Heart-Shaped Frame grudge ends up with a total of 16 points, making it a 4-carat grudge.

6

Why We Hold Grudges – and Why Some People Don't

'Anger as soon as fed is dead – / 'Tis starving makes it fat.'

Emily Dickinson

In the last chapter, I hope I demonstrated to every reader's satisfaction that grudge is all around us: in buildings, birds, political and cultural history, music, architecture. The tendency and urge to hold grudges when we feel we've been hurt or wronged is, I believe, an inescapable part of human nature.

So what about those people, like my husband, who just don't hold grudges – or who try to hold them and then lose them somewhere along the way? In fact, I shall use my husband as an example. He's certainly not an all-embracing spiritual type who mindfully practises and advocates the radical acceptance of whatever life offers. Far from it. He is passionate and opinionated, and can get angry and rail against things, and he regularly says, 'Just tell them to fuck off,' when someone has overstepped the mark and I'm trying to decide how to deal with it.

He *says* that . . . and then he forgets all about it. Which means he's got fewer grudges in his Grudge Cabinet than I have. He has been known to give people (only the richly deserving, mind) a real verbal savaging, whereas I am unfailingly polite and charming even when someone has just bopped me over the head with a hammer. Strange, then, that I'm the champion grudge-holder out of the two of us. I doubt my husband could even find his Grudge Cabinet (assuming it were a real object, which it isn't) if I sent him to look for it. I would have to give him directions. Then, once he'd found the Cabinet, he would need to remind himself of its contents. 'Oh yeah – this!' he would say as he pulled out and examined each grudge.

I, meanwhile, could be blindfolded, wrapped in plastic sheeting and hidden in some shrubbery in Eastbourne, and I'd still be able to find my Grudge Cabinet in three seconds flat, using only my sense of smell to guide me. Which brings us to this all-important question: what makes you the sort of person who is more likely, or less likely, to hold grudges?

Let's look at the relevant factors:

1. Your love of, or need for, stories and storytelling

When something has happened to you that you think is either interesting or remarkable, how strong is your desire to share the story with someone else? I am someone who loves stories. I'm addicted to telling them and to hearing them. One of the things I say most often is, 'Ooh, tell me! Tell me every detail!' My husband would never in a million years ask somebody to tell him 'every detail' of anything. Quite the contrary. He often says, 'Just give me the gist,' by which he means, 'in as few words as possible.'

I will often ask twenty-odd questions at the end of a long and detailed story, because there are still some tiny points that I want to know more about. As Eckhart Tolle points out in *The Power of Now,* if you don't tell yourself the full story in great detail (including the crucial ingredient of who's been shitty to whom) then holding a grudge is impossible.

My husband is someone who makes a point of remembering far fewer stories than I do. Often, when I bring up something that happened to us a few years ago, he will say, 'Oh, yeah! I'd totally forgotten that.' He has almost no grudges, therefore – and those he does have, it's only because I remind him that he has them. Thinking about it, I'm not sure if these grudges ought to count as his, or if I should classify them as mine that I'm keeping on his behalf.

Very often, my husband and I have conversations that go something like this:

ME: I'm going to Exeter for work next week. I'll book a hotel.

HIM: Why don't you stay with Michael and Linda?

ME: Are you serious?

HIM: Yes. Why not? You'd save money.

ME: Remember the *Upside Down in the Doorway* incident?

HIM: Oh, yeah! Didn't . . . *(face contorts with shock and disbelief)* didn't Michael march into your room and turn the light on, waking you up, for no good reason?

ME: Yes.

HIM: And . . . wasn't he looking for his dog who wasn't even lost? Who was in the next room?

ME: Yes.

HIM: Shit. I'd forgotten that.

ME: I know. I hadn't, though.

HIM: Did that really happen?

ME: Yes.

HIM: Oh. Yeah, definitely book a hotel, then.

Each grudge we hold is a story we tell ourselves, and file away for safe keeping in our memory-anthology of grudge stories. Perhaps we tell these stories to others too. People like me, who love, remember and live by stories, are far more likely to hold grudges than people who live very much in a 'now' that is not informed by a 'past-then' or a 'future-then'. Which leads me neatly to number 2 . . .

2. Your tendency to live in the present moment, with no thoughts of past or future

My husband is Mr Present Moment all the way. To demonstrate what I mean by this, I'm going to show you the contrast between what I'm doing today and what he is doing today.

What I'm Doing Today
<u>Me</u>: I'm having a lovely day sitting in a gorgeous room at Lucy Cavendish College in Cambridge, writing this book. The room has stained-glass windows, views of the most stunning landscaped gardens and trees, and is full of beautiful furniture and art. I've opened two windows and the sun is streaming in, but it's still nice and cool in this room. I'm working on this book, so I'm thinking about lots of things that happened to me in the past. I'm also thinking about the future. The book has to be handed in in a week's time, in order to be published in November 2018 in the UK and January 2019 in the USA. So, here I am, loving this present moment writing in these lovely surroundings, but also thinking about both the past and the future. My present moment is like the perfect pair of curtains: amazing material on the surface (the now) but also enhanced by two layers of lining (the past and the future).

What My Husband is Doing Today
<u>My husband</u>: My husband is also sitting in a beautiful room, in our house. He's got his feet up on the sofa, a cup of coffee by his side, the weekend papers all around him, the TV on, his phone in his hand. He's chilling out. When I left this morning, he told me he didn't have anything planned for

today apart from more chilling out. First thing next Friday, he has a new art exhibition opening, and before it opens he needs to tidy his studio and turn it into a gallery, then hang all the paintings and put all the prints in racks. All of this will take approximately six hours to sort out, at a rough guess. My husband is not planning to use the six free hours he has today to do this work. Why? Because he's simply not thinking about what needs to happen before next Friday morning. That thought *is not in his head at all*.

Other thoughts that aren't in his head at all include: 'Tomorrow morning I'm setting off to Yorkshire to visit my family. When I get back on Wednesday, I'll have to take my son to the orthodontist straight away, and by the time I get back it will be around 4 p.m. and I'll be too tired to tidy the gallery and hang paintings. I can't hang paintings on Thursday either, because it's the End of Term Service at the kids' school, and then we're going out for dinner with friends . . . so in fact, if I don't hang the paintings and sort the gallery out today, there will be no other time for me to do it. And Sophie won't be able to step in and do it for me, because her grudge book has to be delivered on Friday and she's working full-time on that.'

The above is an example of a future-infused thought that my husband might potentially have in the present moment, but is not having. A past-infused thought he might have, but also is not having, is: 'I remember that Sophie and I discussed when the best time would be for me to sort out the gallery, and we agreed that the *only* time for me to do it would be Saturday 30 June. I then said, "Okay, I'll tackle it first thing on Saturday." And so, now that it's Saturday, I will.'

I believe that if Eckhart Tolle ever met my husband, he would want to scoop him up and take him on tour with him as the perfect, shining example of how to live in the moment. My husband isn't thinking *at all* about how what he does today might affect the successful opening of his exhibition on Friday morning, and I'm trying to follow in his enlightened footsteps by not worrying about it either.

I hope you can see how being more like my husband in this respect, and less like me, would make a person less likely to hold grudges.

3. Whether you prefer to tackle negative experiences head-on, and form a 'pessimism of strength', or whether you prefer simply not to think about anything negative or upsetting

When I published my second crime novel, *Hurting Distance*, which contains some upsetting violence, a woman approached me after I'd done an event to promote the book and said, angrily, 'Why do you write about horrible things?' She told me she hadn't enjoyed my book and preferred to read novels in which nothing too distressing happened. I told her that I was the opposite: *because* distressing things do happen in the world, and had happened to me, I wanted and needed to write stories in which people go through unpleasant experiences and survive them, and come out stronger. 'That's silly,' she said. 'Just don't write about them. Write about happy things.'

If you agree more with me here than with her, then you're more likely to form and hold grudges than she is. She can't bear to think about anything unpleasant, and is therefore more likely to try to forget any incident that angers or upsets her as soon as the moment has passed. Indeed, after telling me how much she had disliked my book, she gave me a hug and said, 'But I really like *you*, even though I hated your book,' so she evidently didn't bear a grudge against me for having written a book that had upset her. She wanted and needed a happy ending, in real life as well as in fiction.

4. How meticulous/precise or absent-minded/chaotic you are

Meticulous and precise people are better at maintaining any kind of collection than chaotic people, including collections of grudges. My friend Nicky is seriously absent-minded. Over the years, she has lost many wallets, credit cards, sleeping bags and items of clothing. If we're in a hotel and she says, 'I'm packed and ready to go,' I always say, 'Let me check your room.' She always does, because we both know that I will find enough of her clothes still in wardrobes and drawers or stuffed under the bed to open a small fashion shop if I were so inclined.

Nicky regularly mislays or forgets her grudges, as she does her possessions. Then she's hurt all over again by each new encounter with friends, relatives and acquaintances who have harmed her in the past. 'He was such a selfish wanker to me!' she will protest tearfully, having forgotten that this has happened five times before at least.

5. What you believe about whether it's right or wrong to hold grudges

As we've discussed already, many of us have acquired the idea that it's mean-spirited and petty to hold grudges. So we try not to, and some of us succeed. My children, by contrast, have grown up in a home where holding grudges is seen as a natural part of life. My daughter doesn't feel bad about having a grudge collection of her own. The other day she said to me, 'I'm friendly with Millie to keep the peace at school, Mum, but I never forget that she's a massive bum-crack.' (This is my daughter's insult of choice, and one she invented. Yes, I am very proud of her.)

This grudge acts as a very efficient protective shield. When Millie has a 'bad day' (a day on which her unhappiness prompts her to gaslight my daughter relentlessly for hours), my daughter doesn't let it get to her at all. She walks through the door and says quite happily, 'Millie was *awful* today, the bum-crack,' and then goes on to have a perfectly nice evening. Her grudge is a bookmark in her mind, telling her, 'Remember, this is what Millie does. You know this, and expect no different or better. And she isn't getting away with it, because you have a grudge about this that testifies to the not-okay-ness of Millie's behaviour, and that contains a resolution to avoid Millie as soon as the two of you are no longer at the same school.'

Each time Millie behaves obnoxiously, my daughter is neither surprised nor upset, because she hasn't made the mistake of wiping the slate clean in her mind. A clean slate can be dirtied again and again by a person incapable of behaving well, and who wants to keep pointlessly wiping? Instead, frame that dirty slate and put it in your Grudge Cabinet!

Imagine if every child had a mother who said (and indeed published) mottos like 'Frame that dirty slate and put it in your Grudge Cabinet!' Wouldn't the world be a much better place? I think so. More people would be rightfully proud of their good grudges, like my daughter is, because they would understand that grudges can and should be great – for the grudge-holder and also for the world at large.

6. How easy we find it to express our feelings openly

Remember Carol, from Rebecca's 'ruined' birthday dinner (Chapter 3, grudge type no. 1, Unprovoked Attack Grudge)? Having told Rebecca that she was crazy and ought to fuck off, Carol felt no need to bear a grudge. People who find it easy to express their anger and negative reactions spontaneously and in the moment often feel no need to hold grudges. Grudges are more likely to bloom in the minds of those of us (me included; me especially) who find it impossible to express negative feelings openly and without fear of reprisals. Grudges are a way to make you feel you're taking a stand, even if only in your thoughts, when you're too afraid to take a public stand.

Here is a confession for you, folks: I am forty-seven years old, and I have never expressed my anger in a spontaneous way. The most I might say is, 'You know when you did X? I mean, sorry to bring it up, and I might be being silly, but could you maybe in future . . .' This is the way I speak even when I am burning with rage inside. Am I stupidly repressed, or laudably diplomatic and considerate? This crucial topic – how best to respond when someone gives you cause to hold a new grudge – will be covered in Chapter 11: How to Be A Responsible Grudge-Holder. For present purposes, it's enough to observe that if you're someone who can open your mouth and yell, 'Leave me alone, you bully!' when the occasion demands it, and then feel that, as a result, justice has been done, then you're unlikely to need grudges, me or this book. (Though you might enjoy reading on anyway, to gain insight into how the other half lives. And I would argue – and I will, in Chapter 11 – that you should do less yelling and cursing and more enlightened grudge-holding for a more peaceful life.)

If you're a people-pleaser (someone who prioritises not upsetting others over being true to yourself and speaking and living your own truth) then you are unlikely to feel comfortable yelling, 'Leave me alone, you bully', or even mumbling a much milder, 'Excuse me, but I think you're being a little unreasonable.' People-pleasers feel more comfortable saying, 'Oh, of course, I'd be delighted to do whatever you think is best,' and then holding a massive grudge. It's obvious why. The person we're afraid of upsetting can't see our secret, silent grudge, so we're safe.

Brooke Castillo of The Life Coach School calls such people-pleasers liars. When I first heard her say this, I can't tell you how relieved I felt. I felt like cheering. Why? Because I used to be precisely that sort of liar. Until the age of roughly thirty-eight, I pretty much told the people I was afraid of exactly what they wanted to hear, while leading a secret double life in which I did what I wanted, irresponsibly and without care for my own safety or well-being. Then I came up against a lie I simply couldn't bring myself to tell (for more detail about this, see the grudge story *The Bellowing in the Kitchen* later in this book) and everything changed. I was intelligent enough (and had imbibed enough self-help books with titles like *When Are You Going To Grow a Spine and Stand*

Up To That Oppressive Twat?) to feel sickened by the prospect of yet another capitulation on my part for the sake of peace. So, I resisted. With as much charm and tact as I could muster, I openly stated that I disagreed with The Person I Most Feared in the World (TPIMFITW). I had never done this before – not over anything major that I knew would cause a problem.

The predictable anger and attempts at emotional blackmail followed, but I managed to stand firm because I was certain I'd done and said the right thing. However, not everybody agreed that I had. Apart from me and TPIMFITW, there were other people who were involved in the story. All of them were scared of TPIMFITW too – some more than I was, and some less so. All of them questioned and/or criticised my new behaviour (telling the truth, as I saw it, and saying how I honestly felt about the situation). One said, 'I honestly wonder whether all your therapy and self-help books might be doing you more harm than good.'

Although I stuck to my guns, there was a voice in my head and there is *still* sometimes a voice in my head that whispers, 'But what if you *were* disloyal and unsupportive? What if you *are* a basic-fact-denier, distorter of historical truths and aider and abetter of bad guys?' (These were all things that TPIMFITW said or implied about me after I disagreed with him openly about something that really mattered to him.)

When I hear Brooke Castillo say, over and over again, that people-pleasers are liars, it reminds me that I did the right thing when I tried to tell the truth, however uncomfortable it might have been for certain people. According to Brooke, when you tell people what they want to hear, then even if they like you and approve of you, it's not the real you they're liking or approving of – and so their endorsement is worthless. It's based on a lie.

I find Castillo's theory impossible to disagree with. I now try very hard – tactfully, and always careful to sound as non-confrontational as possible – to say what I really think, even when I'm scared. There's no doubt in my mind, though, that if you're someone who finds it impossible to say how you truly feel because of fear, you're far more likely to acquire a large grudge collection. Many of these, unprocessed, might be tightly wrapped in resentment and hurt. In Chapter 8, we will look at how to remove the negative feelings that might be doing harm to the grudge-holder, to leave only the enlightening and helpful part of the grudge that's worth keeping.

7. How powerful or powerless you feel

Some of us – the lucky ones – feel that we are able adequately to protect ourselves, practically and emotionally, from the adverse effects of living in the world alongside other human beings. Many of us, however, feel constantly at risk of interference, bullying, manipulation, imposition and other unpleasant encroachments. If we are in the second category, we are likely to hold more grudges. Insofar as grudges offer protection (and I firmly believe they do), category 2 people are obviously going to feel they need more protection.

In the opinion of psychologist Tony Ferretti in a piece in *MEL* magazine: 'Sometimes we hold on to grudges because we lack the self-confidence and conflict resolution skills to effectively work through our negative emotions. We may choose to lash out or shut down rather than communicate assertively.'

Until you develop the necessary skills to protect yourself no matter how other people are behaving, you *will* need more protection and grudges are very useful for this purpose. They remind us that, though we might feel powerless, it is nevertheless *not acceptable* that we were treated badly.

As I've said: I felt powerless until I was thirty-eight and first decided to prioritise speaking the truth over and above pleasing TPIMFITW. (I think this name should be pronounced Ta-pim-fit-oo-w; let me know if you disagree.) Now, I no longer feel powerless, but I still hold grudges – in a different way and for different reasons. I'll say more about this in Chapters 8 and 11.

8. Whether you are now or have ever been in an oppressive situation

If you have ever suffered bullying, tyranny or oppression, you are more likely to fear that this will happen to you again. My husband and I often joke about my tendencies in this direction. Sometimes he will say something innocuous like, 'Are you sure you want to set off on an American book tour three days after getting back from an Australian book tour?' and I will start huffing and puffing and saying, 'I know what I want, okay? I'm a free agent and I can and will do *exactly* what I want. Stop trying to control and oppress me!' Very soon we're both laughing about it, because we know why I've reacted like this and that it has nothing to do with my husband or what he said.

If I say to my husband, 'Are you sure you want to do X

or Y?', he never launches into an unhinged rant, because oppression by a narcissistic control freak is something he's never experienced – not for a single day of his life.

If you've been tyrannised or wounded in a particular way in the past, you're more likely to develop grudges in situations that remind you of those original, upsetting situations.

9. How certain or uncertain you tend to be

When I last went to have my eyes tested, my optician told me that I was an ideal eye-testee. 'Your answers are so definitive and precise,' he said. 'You always seem to know the exact answer.'

'That's because you're asking about *my* eyes,' I told him. 'Of course I know whether I can see the bottom row of letters clearly.'

'You'd be amazed how many people don't,' he said. 'Lots of my clients say, "What do you mean by 'clearly'?" Or they say "Yes. Wait, no. I'm not sure."'

When something happens that wounds or enrages us, some of us know, instantly, that something wrong or hurtful has occurred, of which we were the victim. Others immediately start to doubt their right to feel what they feel, and to question whether their memories and impressions are accurate. They tell themselves that maybe the person didn't mean to harm them.

Believing that you can see the facts of the story clearly, and knowing for sure that someone has behaved badly towards you, is obviously more conducive to grudge-holding than doubting everything, from the other person's level of culpability to your own recollections of the event.

10. How changeable or stable your view of the world/ past events is

Some of us feel differently, day to day, about the unchanging facts of our lives and life stories. My friend Lucy is like this. One day she might say, 'My dad's not so bad. He does his best and that's the important thing.' Then, a few days later, she will say, 'I'm not bothering with my dad from now on. He doesn't give a shit about anyone but himself.' It doesn't bother her at all that there's no continuity – she is happy to think well of her father one day and badly the next. Her temperament is therefore not ideally suited to grudge-holding, which inevitably involves the ability to form conclusions about events and people and then stick to them.

11. The extent to which you trust your own judgement

How sure are you that you've been wronged, and that you're not the one in the wrong? As a child and teenager, my natural impulse was always to assume everything was my fault – to apologise, make allowances and change myself so that I didn't have to object to the objectionable behaviour of others (though this attempt to fool myself led to many rebellious moments in which I thought, 'No, this is your fault and I hate you!').

I can't remember precisely how old I was when I decided to trust my own judgement on a more regular and, indeed, semi-permanent basis, but once I did, I got much better at holding grudges, I'm pleased to say. This was many years before I was brave enough to let the world at large *see* that I trusted my own judgement, but it was an important step along the way.

12. How naturally forgiving you are, and how afraid you are of that tendency in yourself

This is a counterintuitive one. There is a strong streak of 'naive doormat' in me. I am, naturally, a happy, positive, affectionate person who loves to love people. About the people in my life who have done me serious emotional harm, I constantly think, 'Maybe I should abandon my grudges about them, fully trust them and totally love them again? Maybe it would be okay and safe to do that?'

In fact, it would be neither okay nor safe. Naïve saps like me need our grudges to protect us; we need them more than most – certainly more than those who genuinely stop liking and caring about those who hurt them, and are never tempted to give second, third and fourth chances.

It is no surprise that I'm a dedicated and proficient grudge-holder. I love stories and storytelling; I prefer to confront negative feelings and experiences and form a 'pessimism of strength'; I believe it's not wrong for me to have grudges – on the contrary, I know it's beneficial; I am meticulous and precise; I have felt powerless for much of my life and still often do; I have found it very difficult, and still do, to express any sort of negative feeling openly; I have been in oppressive situations where I've felt tyrannised and bullied; I tend to feel certain that my version of the story is accurate, and I trust my own judgement; I am stable, not changeable; I am instinctively forgiving and just want to love and trust everyone, and I know this could put me at risk.

The above description might fit you too. Or you might

be very different from me in all these respects. If you are, I suspect your behaviour and tendencies with regard to grudges and grudge-holding will be very different from mine, which is absolutely fine. We're all different, and the most important thing is that we shouldn't blame ourselves for how we've turned out. Deciding to change your behaviour and beliefs is great if that's what you want to do – I wanted to become less of a people-pleaser and feel more empowered, and I succeeded in doing this – but I don't for a second blame myself for being a scared people-pleaser (liar) for thirty-eight years. For the way I felt before I was able to take charge of my emotional state and change it, I assign full responsibility to all the people in my life who should have been less terrifying. Take that, scarers!

Now I have a great 5-carat grudge to share with you. This one's a selfie – one of the most powerful grudge types.

The House In Amsterdam
Grudge type: no. 16, Selfie Grudge – a grudge you hold against yourself

Four of us – me, my boyfriend (who later became my husband) and our friends Ewan and Paula – had got into a routine of going on holiday together. We'd done it several times over the years, and several 'holiday norms and routines' had developed. One of these was that we didn't split off into couples; we spent every day and evening together. It was unheard of, on our holidays, for one of us to say, 'I want to walk up Mount Whatnot today, and you guys want to go to the painted cave, so I'll just go off on my own and do my thing, and I'll meet you later for dinner.' Any such comment would have been viewed by Ewan and Paula as unfriendly and unsociable. Ewan in particular would have been hurt if he'd thought my boyfriend and I might not want to hang out with him and Paula as a foursome all the time.

One year we went on holiday to Amsterdam. We all wanted to look round lots of art galleries, and go out for nice meals and drinks, so that was uncontroversial. Ewan and Paula also very much wanted to see the Anne Frank house.

At this time in my life, I had had no experience of planning my own holidays. Zero. I'd gone from being a child who went on holidays planned by my parents, to being a very new adult who went on holidays organised by Ewan and Paula, or by my boyfriend's mother and stepfather. Although I was over eighteen and legally a grown-up, it didn't occur to me that I should be entirely free to choose what I did or didn't do on holiday – especially on a holiday with other people, where one might need to compromise.

I very much did not want to go to the Anne Frank house. Although I hadn't yet grown brave enough to tell the truth about my thoughts and feelings, I have always had strong views about what I do and don't want to do on holiday. Since I was about six, all I've really wanted to do on holiday is swim in the sea, swim in a swimming pool, read on a sunlounger, eat nice food and drink nice drinks, and that's it. I do love art galleries, so I'm happy to look round the occasional one, and I also like shops. I'm happy to go to the cinema or the theatre while on holiday, as long as it doesn't take away from my beach or pool time.

Here's something I don't want, have never wanted and will never want to do on holiday: go to a house associated specifically and exclusively with the genocidal murder of an innocent teenage girl, and immerse myself in thoughts of the horrors she must have suffered.

All the way to Amsterdam, the idea that I had to go to the Anne Frank house on the second afternoon of my week's holiday (Ewan had drawn up a detailed schedule of our activities), and probably spend at least two hours there, depressed me and took the shine off the whole trip. Even after we'd been there and done it, and it was crossed off the schedule, I was still depressed and couldn't enjoy the nice bits of the holiday. I felt sickened by my own cowardice. I was clever enough to be well aware that I had not *had to* go to the Anne Frank house at all.

I would have been perfectly within my rights to say to Ewan and Paula, 'Hey, listen, I don't want to do this, so I'll hang out in a bar and come and meet you once you've finished here.' I imagined myself saying those words, knowing that there was absolutely no chance I'd actually be brave enough to say them.

I already knew that I was a coward, but this was a situation where the stakes were relatively low, and I really should have been able to muster the courage to say, 'I don't want to do this and so I'm not going to.' Ewan would have sulked, but so what? I could have said, 'Look, it's unreasonable of you to be angry about this. I'm joining in with every single other item on the schedule – all forty-seven of them.'

I didn't say it. I didn't say any of what I wanted to say. Instead, I went to the Anne Frank house so as not to annoy Ewan. It was the wrong thing to do – it didn't benefit me and it certainly didn't benefit Ewan. Years later, once I'd become a bit braver, I sometimes said and did things for no other reason than to annoy Ewan, because I was resentful about failing to annoy him when I should have, when my motivating impulse would have been nobler than simply, 'I owe Ewan some annoyance, so what can I say that'll annoy him?'

I haven't been on holiday with Ewan and Paula since Amsterdam. Once, some years later, Ewan said, 'We should go on holiday together again – why don't we do that any more?' I said, 'Yes, we must,' and then made sure not to arrange it. I said, 'I don't know why we don't do it any more,' though I knew perfectly well: I wouldn't have had the courage to stand up to Ewan, should he happen to suggest some holiday activity that I very much did not want to do.

I hold this grudge about my own cowardice in order to remind myself that it's up to me to make sure I don't agree to do something I know I will hate.

GRADING *THE HOUSE IN AMSTERDAM* GRUDGE:

1. Was the intention of the grudgee **(me)**:

a) definitely or probably bad

b) possibly bad

c) not bad (1 point)

2. Did they know they were upsetting, hurting or being unfair to you?

a) Yes, definitely (3 points)

b) Possibly

c) Not at all

3. Was the overall situation:

a) very serious

b) quite serious

c) not very serious (1 point)

4. Was the effect upon you of what they did or said:

a) very bad – it allowed me to continue people-pleasing (lying), not living my truth, putting my own deepest needs and strongest wishes in a subservient position to what someone else thought should happen. It was a betrayal of myself. (3 points)

b) quite bad

c) not so bad

5. Should or could they have known/done better?

a) Yes

b) **Maybe – I** *did* **know better, but in my state of fear and cowardice, I wasn't capable of doing better at that point in my life. (2 points)**

c) No

6. Did they cause you real harm?

a) **Yes – if I'd stood up to Ewan on that occasion, that could have been the beginning of the end of me being terrified to voice my quite reasonable thoughts and wishes. I was eighteen or nineteen at the time; I could have saved myself twenty years of self-betrayal and fear, maybe, if I'd changed the pattern by speaking up in this extremely low-stakes situation. (3 points)**

b) Maybe

c) No

7. Is the 'Grrrr!' factor of this grudge:

a) high

b) medium

c) **low – I find it more shocking and sad than 'Grrrr' when I think about this grudge. (1 point)**

8. Have you held this grudge:

a) for ages – since 1990 (3 points)

b) for a medium length of time; or, for a short time and you think you'll hold it for a bit longer but not for ever

c) for a short time, and you'll probably have given up this grudge by next week

My *The House in Amsterdam* grudge has 17 points so far.

9. Would this incident, alone, be sufficient to make you hold a grudge about this person or people?

a) Yes

b) No. Everyone sometimes does something they don't want to do in order to keep someone else happy. If I'd only done this once and it wasn't part of a pattern that was crushing my soul, I'd think it was fine that I'd done it. (minus 1 point)

10. Would something bad or frightening have happened to your grudgee if they *hadn't* performed the grudge-sparking action?

a) No

b) Yes. Ewan would have sulked, turned cold and

found ways to punish me. I would have found this
terrifying and very upsetting. (minus 1 point)

11. Would this grudge be cancelled out/terminated if your
grudgee apologised fully and wholeheartedly?

**a) No. I have forgiven myself, but I still can't help
thinking, 'Even so – it blows my mind that you
didn't know better and do better at the time.' I
still feel that this grudge is a powerful one that
needs to be remembered and kept. (No points
deducted)**

b) Yes

12. Is your grudgee someone who matters to you, and to
whom you matter?

a) Yes, massively

b) Yes, quite a lot (2 points)

c) Not especially

The House in Amsterdam grudge ends up with a total of
17 points, making it a 5-carat grudge.

7

The Grudge-fold Path

'Begin each day by telling yourself: Today I shall be meeting
with interference, ingratitude, insolence, disloyalty, ill-will,
and selfishness – all of them due to the offenders' ignorance
of what is good or evil.'

Marcus Aurelius

Now we're going to look in more detail at how holding
grudges can make you a more forgiving person, however
strange and counter-intuitive that may sound.

It has been well established by medical experts that our
psychological well-being or distress has an impact upon our
physical health. Prolonged states of anger, sadness, fear and
bitterness can cause our physical health to deteriorate. When
we are advised to think happy thoughts, let go of resentment,
move on and forgive, those advising us usually mean well
and are trying to help. They know (as do we, mostly) that
if we allow vengefulness and hatred to fester inside us, we
might soon find we have migraines and skin irritations, sore
throats and stomach aches.

It's important to be aware, though, that there is more than

one kind of resentment, and more than one cause of bitterness. Yes, we might feel furious if someone borrows our bicycle and then sets fire to it instead of returning it, but we might feel even more vengeful if a third party then tells us, 'Don't be angry with your bike-vandal friend, because your anger will only cause *you* pain, and it won't affect him. Forgive him for your *own* sake.'

'What the hell are you on about?' you might think, if you're anything like me. 'Someone sets fire to my bike for a laugh, and I have to immediately forgive him and move on? What if *that's* the thing that's going to make me feel bitter and come out in hives? What if your advice right now, and my attempt to follow it when all my instincts are screaming, "Grudge! Grudge!", is the provocation that's going to give me sore gums and scaly feet?'

(Those are not random examples, my friends. My own attempts to deny my quite natural and justified feelings of anger over the years have led to these very maladies – now cured, I'm pleased to say. My feet are now beautiful and smooth. I'm happy to send a photo if you don't believe me. Hold grudges like I do and you too can have beautiful, smooth feet!)

For many of us, being told to forgive and move on for our own sake, while we're still reeling from whatever it is that some rotter has done to us, feels like a new and separate insult. In contrast, we might feel better almost instantly if instead that third party were to say, 'What an irredeemable, unmitigated arsehole! You know what? Never lend him anything again. Remember if tempted: *he set fire to your bike.*'

(Saying 'What an irredeemable, unmitigated arsehole!', or

the equivalent, is not an impediment to forgiveness or positivity. It's a flamboyant and enjoyable way to let off steam. Don't say it to the offending person – that won't help – but feel absolutely free to say it about them. Once you've insulted them colourfully in the privacy of your own home, you'll feel less pent-up rage towards them.)

If feeling better in our minds is likely to make us healthier in our bodies, and most medical experts would agree that it is, then why do we hear so much, 'Look, just forget it, move on and think positive' and not so much, 'He did that? That's definitely grudgeworthy. You need and deserve a grudge about this that you can keep for ever'? The reason, I believe, is that many, many people simply don't care that something horribly upsetting or unjust was done to you, and they want their lives to be made easier by you agreeing not to care about it either.

Please don't feel worse now because I've told you that your loved ones don't care when bad things happen to you. It's nothing personal against you. They also, most of them, don't regard it as deserving of commemoration when bad things happen to *them*. So many large and small terrible things happen in the world, daily, that many of us believe we *have* to keep moving right along, almost as if we haven't noticed, or else we'd be consumed by bile and bitterness all the time. That's because most people don't yet know about The Grudge-fold Path, and don't understand that grudges aren't an impediment to feeling happy, putting positive energy into the world and forgiving those who have treated us poorly.

Once we start to follow the Grudge-fold Path, we demonstrate clearly – with our willingness to form grudges and our pride in doing so – that we care about and are unwilling to brush aside some of the most important landmarks in our emotional and psychological history. The by-product of this change will be that, gradually, we will find ourselves increasingly willing and able to acknowledge the need to honour these emotional-history landmarks in the lives of others too. When your friend Betty says, 'Forget it and move on,' she's not trying to compound your pain; she is simply passing on the received non-wisdom that has no doubt been inflicted upon her hundreds of times in her life already. Once we give ourselves permission to care in a serious way about how *we* are treated, most of us will automatically start to extend that care to others.

Whenever a friend or acquaintance tells me that somebody has mistreated them, I clear a space in my day and say, 'Tell me every detail.' Then I listen. Once I've heard the story, I almost always agree that, yes, the teller has been mistreated and has every right to feel as they do. I say, 'That is definitely not okay. I would hold a grudge about that.' I explain that I don't mean they should yell at the person, cut them out of their life, hate them, never forgive them. I simply mean, 'This is grudgeworthy. A commemorative grudge story is required – one that you should remember for as long as it's useful to you, and feel free to tell whenever you want to.' When someone hears another person say, 'The bad thing that happened to you really matters,' they feel a little better straight away. Psychotherapist Helen Acton agrees: 'Much of the healing power of psychotherapy is in the therapist's readiness to "bear witness" to the experience of the client, as the client reports it. For a client to be heard, seen, empathised with and validated – to have the sense that their experience and their feelings about that experience *matter* – can be transformative. For Sophie and others who hold grudges, the grudge can provide a means of bearing witness to *oneself*. Even if the grudge story is never told, to treasure it in a Grudge Cabinet is to say "This matters, I matter, my feelings matter and I will hold that truth for myself".'

Most people need to feel the negative feelings that have arisen inside them first, and let those feelings pass in a natural way, before they can move on and feel positive again – and there's nothing wrong with that. People who tell us to forgive and move on when we're not ready to do so, or who tell us, 'Don't think bad things about X, think good things about her' often leave us with the impression that they're more on the side of the person who has harmed us than they are on our side, or that they simply can't be bothered to waste their time and energy dealing with our pain or anger, and so they'd like us to get over it and cheer up because then they would be less inconvenienced. The trouble is, we can't 'move on' or forgive at the click of someone's fingers. Things happen, and we feel the way we feel about them.

Brooke Castillo is quite open about the fact that she still sometimes finds herself trapped in a state of rage, or crying several times during a weekend spent surrounded by her extended family. She knows all the theory of how to make sure we don't cede our power to others and instead to take charge of our emotional lives ourselves, but she also admits that she's not perfect and that she sometimes can't manage straight away to put the brilliant theory into practice.

Eckhart Tolle, in contrast, never once in *The Power of Now* says, 'I must admit, all this theory I wholeheartedly believe in totally went out of the window last week when my neighbour yelled, "Oy, mate, I've seen better gurus than you in my dustbin!" over the garden fence. I picked up a rock and hurled it at the bastard's head. Even I can't be guru-like all the time!' Tolle's writings convey the firm impression that no provocation, however huge, could induce him to behave in what he calls an 'unconscious' manner.

I find it extremely reassuring to know that both Eckhart Tolle and Brooke Castillo exist. I love the idea of the perfectly enlightened guru – it's nice to know that at least one person has managed to get beyond the stuff that annoys most of us on a daily basis and simply never gets irritated any more. It is, therefore, humanly possible, though it probably will never be possible for most ordinary people like you and me, so perhaps we shouldn't waste time trying. I love equally the idea of a wise, strong woman who, nevertheless, sometimes finds herself in the grip of uncontrollable negative emotions.

I can practise what both Tolle and Castillo preach up to a point, but I also felt the need to formulate an approach that would work for me beyond that point – a way forward in a world in which other people regularly and seriously upset and annoyed me. Every time I heard Castillo say, 'No one can hurt your feelings unless you let them', and every time I heard Tolle say (for instance) 'Tell yourself a different story in which someone *didn't* try to kill your dog', I found myself thinking, 'Hmm. But . . . But . . . they *can*. They *did*.'

That's why I invented The Grudge-fold Path, which is both enlightened and realistic. The Grudge-fold Path takes for granted – takes as its absolute, unarguable starting point and foundation – the unchanging fact that people, intentionally and unintentionally, will regularly hurt, inconvenience and infuriate us throughout our lives, unless we go and live in a cabin in some remote woods, with no WiFi and miles from all other human beings.

That's right, folks. People *can* piss you off. They *will* piss you off. They'll betray you, insult you, take you for granted, slander you, forget to pay you back after promising they would, set fire to your bike, buy the exact same skirt you bought without first asking you if you'd mind. I'd be thrilled to be proved wrong about this, but I strongly suspect Other People will *always* do all the bad things they've done in the past, and all the remaining bad things they've not yet tried.

Accepting that people can and will hurt and annoy us for as long as there is human life on this or any planet is a great starting point. The next question is: what do we do about it, so that we don't suffer any more than we have to, and to try to ensure that there is some justice in our lives and in the world?

The answer is simple: we follow the Grudge-fold Path. This involves neither clinging to anger and bitterness so that they ruin our lives and the lives of others nor forgiving everybody straight away, forcing ourselves to think only positive thoughts (sugar-coating) or trying to repress our understandable and justified hurt or rage. The Grudge-fold Path cuts a sensible and satisfying middle way between the two extremes.

When I put this to Anne Grey, she said, 'I agree that sugar-coating, pretending and denying are unhelpful. To live a life that's focused on the positive, or what uplifts you, does not require denial. In fact the opposite is true: it requires you to be more authentic, more true to you. Instead of denying your situation, it can be helpful to see it clearly, and accept your thoughts and emotions about it as they are without judgement, with love and acceptance. This is naturally uplifting, and frees you to speak and act wisely.'

I will now take you through, step by step, what following the Grudge-fold Path means in practice.

The Ten Tenets of the Grudge-fold Path

Tenet 1: We understand that people can and will piss us off and upset us, always and for ever.

Tenet 2: As a result, we will sometimes experience negative emotions, such as anger and sadness. We must not try to deny or banish these feelings, or move them along too quickly. We will absolutely reject any suggestion that it is mean or unforgiving of us to have these feelings.

Tenet 3: We will not cling to these negative feelings and resolve to make them a permanent and defining part of who we are. We will recognise that anger, sadness and all negative feelings can pass, however strongly we feel them in the moment.

Tenet 4: We understand that the need to make something lasting out of what happened to us *does not mean* that we must and should feel bad for ever, or make the person who hurt us feel bad, or take revenge on them. We should not mistakenly attach our need for something lasting (commemoration of the important thing that happened to us) to our negative feelings or to any harmful, aggressive or retaliatory actions. (These are always wrong.)

Tenet 5: We understand that the need to make something lasting out of what happened to us will be fulfilled by the creation of a grudge about the sparking incident – one that will harm neither ourselves nor our grudgee/s.

Tenet 6: Before we create our grudge, we must prepare a Grudge Cabinet. Whatever form our Grudge Cabinet is going to take, we need to get it ready to receive.

Tenet 7: We must then create our grudge (how to do this is covered in Chapter 8), and process it to make sure it's valid, harmless and psychologically beneficial in the lessons it teaches us and the positive values it reinforces in us.

Tenet 8: We will then grade and classify our grudge, and place it in an optimal position in our Grudge Cabinet.

Tenet 9: Once we have performed all of the actions described above, the importance of what happened has been acknowledged and commemorated. At that point – and this will sound unlikely but I swear to you, it really works – we will, almost always, realise that the negative feelings sparked by the inciting incident are no longer useful to us and disappear quite spontaneously. *Now* we can forgive without fear that an offence against us will be lost in the mists of history with nothing to show that it ever happened. *Now* we can move on, in a way we wouldn't have been able to if we hadn't been creative and built our commemorative grudge; if instead we'd tried to force ourselves to think nice thoughts and forgive too soon, without any recognition that the hurt or offence we'd suffered mattered to anybody.

Tenet 10: We will repeat the above process as often as we find ourselves on the receiving end of grudge-sparking incidents. We will hold our grudges responsibly and safely until such time as we decide to let a particular grudge or grudges go. That might be never, which is absolutely fine. We will trust that The Grudge-fold Path will protect us (as much as it's possible to be protected in this world) from pain, rage, and the feeling that injustices against us have gone unrecognised. We will henceforth view (good, valid, responsibly-held) grudges not as shameful but as great, necessary, empowering and enlightening.

That's all there is to it – it's simple, effective and will work as well for you as it has for me. When I explain this to people, I am always asked the same question first:

'What if my negative feelings don't shift?'

If you have made your grudge, processed it, learned from it and put it in your Cabinet and you find you're still incandescent with rage, here's what you should do: accept that feeling, and don't worry about it. Say to yourself, 'Welcome, anger. You have every right to be here. Stay as long as you want.' Eventually the feeling will shift and all that will be left is the pride and joy bestowed upon you by your grudges, which will sit in your Cabinet like gold medals for wartime bravery.

Helen Acton says, 'Sophie's approach acknowledges another psychotherapeutic tenet, articulated most famously by Carl Rogers, father of person-centred psychotherapy – "the curious paradox is that when I accept myself just as I am, then I can change". What therapists know to be true is that feelings are messengers, and the more we push those messengers down or away, the harder and louder they knock at the door. Welcome them in! Hear their message! Sooner or later they will quieten down and move on.'

I've said this already, but I'm going to repeat it because I want everyone to take it in: my negative feelings caused by grudge-sparking incidents are 100 times weaker, and shift 100 times quicker, since I've been following The Grudge-fold Path. I'm so busy thinking, 'Ooh – a new grudge! I can't wait to process, classify and grade it!' that I often manage to skip the hurt/anger part altogether. Note, though, that it has taken several years for me to get to this point. Please don't expect the Grudge-fold Path to work like magic straight away. Instead, notice that the first grudge you consciously and joyfully create to put in your Cabinet makes the negative feelings pass *just a little more quickly*. Each time you follow the steps, the effect will become a little more noticeable, and I believe that most of you, like me, will in due course find that those negative feelings soon start to appear in weaker, more transient forms – if they manifest at all.

When you're sitting inside your house and see a huge wasp buzzing on the other side of the firmly closed windows, you don't flinch and worry about being stung, do you? Even if you're seriously allergic to wasp stings, you don't panic. That's because you know for certain that the panes of glass are protecting you. This is how I've felt since I've consciously followed the Grudge-fold Path: protected.

HOW CAN GRUDGES BE GOOD FOR YOU?

— By acting as commemorative objects whose function is to testify that the wrong that was done to you/the wound you sustained matters, that it will never be okay that it happened and that you are entitled to feel your feelings caused by the sparking incident for as long as feels right to you.

— By remaining as a presence in your life that will remind you of the valuable lessons you learned, of how you do and don't want to behave in future and of who you need to protect yourself against and/or develop firmer boundaries with.

— By acting as a motivating force. My friend Jill, a Booker-Prize-shortlisted novelist, resolved to use her talents and brains to achieve great things after being told by a teacher at the Catholic school she attended, 'Jill, there's no such beatitude as "Blessed are the clever".'

Helen Acton agrees that grudges can be powerful motivators: 'Many grudge-holders use them as a motivator. It's not uncommon for someone who has been treated badly as a child to find the memory of it – the grudge they have about it – empowering in later life. "I'll show them!" They may feel fired up by it, filled with a positive revengeful energy that inspires some of their best work.'

HOW CAN HOLDING GRUDGES MAKE YOU A MORE FORGIVING PERSON?

— Humans are justice-seeking creatures. We don't like the idea of people getting away with wrongdoing. Once your grudge is firmly and happily in place, you will no longer think that your grudgee would get off scot-free if you forgave him. You'd know that he wouldn't have got away with it, because there's your grudge, in the Cabinet, to prove it. You won't feel, therefore, that if you were *now* to forgive and move on, no trace of the ill-treatment you suffered would remain, and there would be nothing to acknowledge that it mattered. You will therefore be more inclined and more likely to forgive.

— The actions you need to perform in order to get the grudge from sparking incident to pride of place in Grudge Cabinet (Tenets 6, 7 and 8 above) will give you something creative to focus on, which will inevitably turn your thoughts in a positive direction and infuse you with positive energy. This might sound utterly implausible to some of you, but I promise you it's true: I have reached the point in my pursuance of the Grudge-fold Path where I'm actually a little delighted and grateful for each new grudge I create – and, by extension, grateful to the people who provide me with the sparking incidents that allow me to create them and learn from them. Once you start to feel that way, you will find yourself feeling more forgiving without even trying.

— Once you've performed the actions necessary for becoming a responsible grudge-holder (these are described in Chapter 11) you'll know that other people might hold as many grudges against you as you hold against them. They're not flawless, perfectly behaved human beings and neither are you. And wouldn't you want to be forgiven, in spite of those commemorative grudges people have about you, instead of cut off or hated for ever? Then, in accordance with the principle of 'do unto others as you would have them do unto you', you will find yourself wanting to forgive more frequently than you do presently.

— Once you're on the Grudge-fold Path, your feelings of anger and pain will no longer be strengthened by your attempts to resist, deny or move on too quickly from those feelings. As Eckhart Tolle says: 'Whatever you fight, you strengthen, and what you resist, persists.' Equally, your negative feelings will not be strengthened in resistance to people telling you to forgive, forget and move on, and whatever you do, make sure not to hold a grudge because that would be bad and wrong. You'll either calmly ignore those people, knowing they're mistaken, or else you'll create a grudge about them that will empower you. Either way, you won't be hoodwinked into believing that you ought to banish or deny your rage and pain – with the result that those emotions won't feel threatened and go into overdrive to assert their right and need to stick around.

Put simply, once you've got your great grudge in place, you will understand that you can now *afford* to forgive, should you so wish – and you'll find that you wish to forgive far more often. I put the word *afford* in italics because I love putting things in italics, but also because I think the analogy with money works well here. Imagine an anonymous bene-factor, tomorrow, gives you a million pounds. Would you think it was okay, and sensible, to spend all of it on a large, beautiful diamond that you've taken a fancy to – every last penny of it? I'm guessing you wouldn't. Most of you would probably think that you should buy a smaller, less valuable diamond and save at least some of the million pounds for mortgage payments, school and university fees, emergencies, a pension fund.

Now imagine that the anonymous benefactor gives you not one million pounds but ten million pounds. In that context, if your heart's greatest desire was to own the massive diamond that costs a million pounds, you might think, 'That's fine. I can afford to buy it. After all, I have *nine* million pounds in my savings account, so I'm safe and covered for all eventualities.'

This is exactly what good grudges do for you: they cover

you and make you safe by offering a learning opportunity, symbolic justice and protection, so that you can afford to forgive if you want to. Your grudge is your savings. It's that cushion you've put aside, so that *something remains*. And that something that remains enables you to feel much happier and more accepting of the idea that the rest (the negative feelings) might not remain. This is how holding grudges enables us to forgive more easily.

In the next chapter, How to Convert Negative Grudge Energy Into Positive Grudge Energy, we're going to look at the importance of storytelling, in relation to our grudge stories, and how we can use it to remove the health-damaging negativity from our grudges once our initial wounded feelings from the sparking incident have passed, leaving only the good stuff, which will improve our lives and benefit the world. We're going to get into the fine detail of what I'm actually suggesting you all should do, and how, precisely, to do it.

Before we take that next step, I'm going to share another of my grudge stories . . .

The Fat Comment
Grudge type: (not previously referenced in this book) – Deliberate Malice Grudge

I was having a conversation with my friend Stella one day, about our old friend Felicity. I hadn't been in touch with Felicity for years, but Stella was friends with her on Facebook and so occasionally told me bits of Felicity-related news. On this occasion, she said, 'I can't believe it – Felicity's got a new girlfriend.'

'Why can't you believe it?' I asked. 'She split up with Marianne two years ago. She was bound to meet someone new eventually.'

Stella gave a hollow laugh. 'Yeah, it's not the finding someone new. It's *who* she's found.'

'And?' I said. 'Who has she found?'

'A woman who's not just ugly, but, like, off the charts ugly.'

'Oh,' I said. I had a feeling something grudgeworthy might be on the way. (It's a sixth sense I have these days: I can sometimes anticipate grudge-sparking incidents before they happen.)

'Yeah,' said Stella. 'I mean . . . you remember how gorgeous Felicity used to be, right?'

'I do,' I said.

Felicity did indeed used to be gorgeous. I hadn't seen her for nearly twenty years, so I had no idea what she looked like now, but I remembered that while she, Stella and I were still a trio of best friends, there was a summer when the three of us went swimming together nearly every day. One day Felicity couldn't make it, and Stella confided to me, 'I actually prefer going swimming with just you. Felicity's got such a gorgeous figure. I feel so inadequate when she's standing next to me, looking all perfect in her swimsuit.'

Clearly, Stella intended for me to be hurt and offended, and feel inadequate myself. When I didn't respond to her remark at all, and instead started chatting cheerfully about something else, she said again, loudly and deliberately, 'Yeah, I prefer going swimming with *just you*, so that I *don't feel inadequate.*'

This backstory is perhaps why I sensed something grudge-worthy was on the way when Stella started to reminisce about how gorgeous Felicity used to be. I was soon proved right. Stella leaned in towards me, so that no one else would hear the comment she was about to make, and said, 'Yeah, I mean, Felicity used to be so attractive, but now she's nearly as fat as this new woman she's dating.'

'Aha!' I thought. 'There it is: a clear and unambiguous attempt to equate fatness with being unattractive, when you're talking to an overweight person.' (The reason this grudge isn't a contender for negligent tactlessness classification is because this was evidently not an accidental or unplanned remark. I could see the glee in Stella's eyes as she was getting ready to make it.)

I chuckled. As a collector of grudges, it's kind of satisfying when you net one that's so deliberately and unequivocally malicious. It must be how fishing enthusiasts feel when they hook a really enormous pike or something. (I don't know anything about fishing, but I'm pretty sure an enormous pike might be a good thing to catch. Please correct me if I'm wrong.)

NOTE: Some readers might by now be thinking, 'Why the hell does Sophie keep so many awful people in her life, who do and say all these dreadful things?' I want to address this question right here, right now. Firstly, though it's possible to banish anyone from your life if you're determined to do so, I much prefer not doing that. I know many cutters-off, and I know that I'm not one by nature, and can never become one. Cutting someone off – saying, 'You've wronged me, so that's it, you're out' – is something I never want to say to anyone if I can help it. Maybe it's cowardice on my part, but it would feel like an unnecessarily violent thing to do.

It seems to me rather like the friendship or relationship equivalent of capital punishment – a thing I am firmly against.

Secondly, most people who do awful things *also* do lovely things. If I cut out everyone who'd ever done or said an awful thing, I would have to cut myself out too. I've made as many mistakes as the next person (I will talk in a later chapter about the importance of acknowledging that other people might have as many grudges about you as you have about other people). Thirdly, it's not so easy to expel someone from your life when you know for certain that ten people still in it, people you care about, would pop up helpfully to say, 'What are you talking about? He's a *lovely* man. He was probably joking when he threatened to poke your eyes out with a kebab skewer. He's got a strep throat at the moment, you know, so don't be too hard on him.'

When you have people in common, it can feel impossible to make a clean break, and the person who stands up to covert bullying, subtle spite or tyrannical-control-disguised-as-loving-concern is often painted as the bad guy.

The key point, though, is this: once you're on the Grudge-fold Path, you will feel the need to cut people out of your life far less often, because your good, responsibly held grudges will protect you from much of the damage they might otherwise do to you.

Anne Grey says, 'When you actively choose to cut someone off, it can feel as though you are carrying that person, or your feelings about this person, with you. By simply making the wise choice that you prefer not to spend time with that person, you are able to be free from them, without carrying the burden of the debilitating emotional charge.'

GRADING *THE FAT COMMENT* GRUDGE:

1. Was the intention of the grudgee **(Stella)**:

a) definitely or probably bad (3 points)

b) possibly bad

c) not bad

2. Did they know they were upsetting, hurting or **being rude to** you?

a) Yes, definitely (3 points)

b) Possibly

c) Not at all

3. Was the overall situation:

a) very serious

b) quite serious

c) not very serious (1 point)

4. Was the effect upon you of what they did or said:

a) very bad

b) quite bad

c) not so bad – I expect Stella to say things like this from time to time, so I'm neither surprised nor upset when she does. (1 point)

5. Should or could they have known/done better?

a) Yes (1 point)

b) Maybe

c) No

6. Did they cause you real harm?

a) Yes

b) Maybe

c) No (1 point)

7. Is the 'Grrrr!' factor of this grudge:

a) high

b) **medium – the deliberate malice merits a high Grrrr! factor, but I also find this grudge very entertaining because I suspect that Stella thinks she's messing with my mind in a way that's not obvious, when in fact it's as obvious as if she were to wear a large sign saying, 'I want to destroy your confidence'. (2 points)**

c) low

8. Have you held this grudge:

a) for ages

b) for a medium length of time; or, for a short time and you think you'll hold it for a bit longer but not for ever

c) **for a short time. The incident described above happened only last week (just in time for my book deadline – hurrah!) Having said that, I'm going to keep this grudge for ever probably, so . . . (3 points)**

My *The Fat Comment* grudge has 15 points so far.

9. Would this incident, alone, be sufficient to make you hold a grudge about this person or people?

a) Yes

b) No. This comment alone would not be sufficient to convince me that there was deliberate malice involved. I'd have assumed Stella had spoken carelessly, and unwittingly revealed her opinion that overweight people are inherently and necessarily unattractive. Most people, realising they had done that, would take care not to do it in future, so if I assumed that was the case with Stella, I wouldn't feel any need for a grudge. **(minus 1 point)**

10. Would something bad or frightening have happened to your grudgee if they *hadn't* performed the grudge-sparking action?

a) No (so no points deducted)

b) Yes

11. Would this grudge be cancelled out/terminated if your grudgee apologised fully and wholeheartedly?

a) No. Stella is in her early fifties and has read a huge number of books. She's had ample time and opportunity to realise that this is a malevolent way to behave towards one of her best friends. I think I'd want to keep a protective grudge in place, no matter what she said and did in the future (so no points deducted).

b) Yes

12. Is your grudgee someone who matters to you, and to whom you matter?

a) **Yes, massively – or rather, we *should* matter a lot to one another because of our structural positions in each other's lives, and it's only because of stories like the one above that I don't have the feelings to match the structural position, if that makes sense. (4 points)**

b) Yes, quite a lot

c) Not especially

The Fat Comment grudge ends up with a total of 18 points, making it a 6-carat grudge.

8

How to Convert Negative Grudge Energy Into Positive Grudge Energy

"Do I not destroy my enemies when I make them my friends?"

Abraham Lincoln

If I'm saying that grudges are good for you, that surely means that I believe they can make you feel better, right? Yes, I do. They won't necessarily, but they can – if you handle them correctly.

What does that mean? Well, it means you can't just let a raw grudge do its own thing, unattended and unsupervised. Think of a raw grudge as a teenage child. Left to its own devices, would it get up at 7 a.m., put on a nice clean school uniform, eat a healthy breakfast and then go to its Geography lesson? Of course not. It would sleep in till eleven, order a pizza with extra cheese for lunch, then play computer games all afternoon. And while that might be what it wants to do in the moment, that course of action (which your raw grudge might wish to take not only today but every day) is unlikely to be beneficial in the long term, which means that you, that grudge's owner/parent, are going to have to intervene.

A raw grudge is an unprocessed grudge. It's not necessarily a *new* grudge. You can have a grudge for many years, even decades, and it might still be unprocessed; or it might have, without any effort on your part, processed itself naturally so that it's now harming neither you nor anybody else. Perhaps you're even benefiting from it.

You can also have a *processed* grudge that's only a week old. The longer you consciously follow the Grudge-fold Path, the more adept you will become at the quick processing of new grudges. If you have not consciously processed your grudges, it's quite likely that at least some of them are still raw – which means they might still be making you feel bad, and you might be using them in the wrong way.

If this is true for you, please don't beat yourself up about it. Every grudge is at first unprocessed, and nothing in our society (apart from me, now, here in this book) teaches us how to put our grudges through the alteration-and-enhancement process that will allow us to benefit from them and remove the unpleasant, harmful feelings.

Let's look in more detail at what 'raw/unprocessed' and 'processed' mean. I'd like to invite you to bring one of your grudges to mind. Once you've chosen the grudge you want to use for this exercise, ask yourself: is this grudge . . .

P1) one that makes you angry or unhappy, even if it's a satisfyingly self-righteous rage or a masochistically enjoyable form of pain, and/or makes you want to do harm to the grudgee;

P2) one that no longer has a live *emotional* charge (which is very different from the live *relevance* charge that all good, processed grudges have) – you don't have any strong feelings when you think of it, though you might have plenty of thoughts and beliefs about it, and you don't want to harm the grudge;

P3) one that you find instructive, fun or entertaining in some way (it makes you laugh to think about it, or reinforces a positive lesson you've learned, and perhaps you like to tell people about it) and you wouldn't dream of harming the grudge.

P1 grudges can do you harm, and harm others. P2 and P3 grudges cannot. The good news is, it's possible to turn nearly all P1 grudges into P2s or P3s by processing them, and turning negative grudge energy into positive grudge energy.

In order to hold grudges wisely and well, you're going to need to work on two things:

1. your grudges
2. yourself

You can tackle either one first, but I'd recommend starting with some grudge-work, which is why I've deliberately arranged it so that 'How to Be a Responsible Grudge-Holder' (the chapter that discusses the work you'll need to do on and in yourself) is the last chapter in this book. Some of you might be thinking, 'Isn't this the wrong way round? Doesn't it make more sense to work on ourselves first, so that our newly improved selves can then do more effective work on our grudges?'

Maybe. I suspect not. Many of this book's readers are likely to be holding at least a dozen unprocessed grudges. Some of you might have lots more than that. Before I invented the Grudge-fold Path I had hundreds of raw grudges, and I know how I'd have felt if someone had said to me, 'Work on yourself first'. I'd have thought, 'Fuck that. I'm not the problem here. Other people, and what they've done to me over the years, are the problem.'

If you're a holder of many raw and possibly painful grudges, I suspect that being told to work first on yourself, as if you're the problem, will cause you to develop a defiant inner resistance to the teachings of the Grudge-fold Path. That's why I'm doing it this way round: the grudges-first approach. Because you, my friend, are only 0.00001 per cent of the problem and 99.whatever's-left-I'm-rubbish-at-Maths-okay? per cent of the problem is having no choice but to live in a world where other people regularly and comprehensively piss you off.

So, let's do some grudge processing! It might not be true in the world of food, where raw and unprocessed is often seen as being more nutritious than processed items, but with grudges, the opposite is true: the healthy grudges are the fully processed ones. The aim of processing is to turn all P1 grudges into P2s or P3s.

How to Process a Grudge

What you need before you start:

1. a notebook, computer or something else to write on/in

2. time - at first it might take two hours, but once you've had some practice, it should only take an hour per grudge

3. at least one raw grudge

METHOD

1. Write down what happened. It can be as long or short as you like, and written in the first person or the third person, but it should contain all the relevant details of the grudge-sparking incident, and possibly some backstory too. Here's an example of how not to do it:

Zac is such a little shit, I will never forgive the bastard. If I ever get a chance to take my revenge on him, you can bet I will do just that!

The above is not, in fact, a story. It's a description of some thoughts I had about someone called Zac. Who is Zac, in relation to me? You have no idea, because I haven't told you. What did he do to me? Again, you can't possibly answer because I've left out all the details. Here's an example of how to write down a grudge story in an effective way:

Zac Rawse was, briefly, a friend/acquaintance of my son's. With my permission, my son once bought Zac a birthday present online, in Zac's presence. **(So far all of this has been backstory – important for setting the scene, so that you know the context before the grudge-sparking part of the story starts.)** Zac memorised the number of the family card my son used to buy the gift, and then went on to spend nearly £500 on that card without permission. When I found out that Zac had robbed us, I contacted his mother, who spoke to him about it. He denied his crime, and said he had used our card to make these purchases by accident, thinking he was using his own bank card. I didn't believe this for a second but his mother clearly wanted to. Luckily, a good friend of my son's who had spent the past few months hanging round at the same skateboarding park as Zac told me that he had heard Zac, over the past few weeks, say to loads of people, 'Hey, I can get you £100 trainers for only £30.'

It was obvious that Zac wouldn't be making much of a profit on this scheme if he was spending the £100 on each pair of trainers himself. Luckily for him, *I* was the one buying the goods at full price, though I had no idea that I was.

Although I was angry about this, I went to his mother about it and not the police. I imagined how I would feel if Zac were my son; I'd want the chance to deal with it myself in the hope of him avoiding a criminal record. Once his mother confronted him with this witness's testimony about his trainers ruse, Zac knew the game was up, and admitted to deliberate theft and fraud. His mother emailed me and said, 'I'm so sorry. Zac is too. I'm sure he'll write to you soon and apologise.'

He never did. At first I suspected he was too ashamed to communicate with me at all, but I started to doubt the sincerity of his contrition when he began to text my son, daily, saying 'Fuck your mum'. It seemed that he was holding a grudge against me for, as he saw it, getting him into trouble. Occasionally he would introduce a bit of variety by texting 'Your [sic] gay' or 'You fucking faggot', but soon afterwards he would always revert to 'Fuck your mum' or 'Duck your mum' (damn autocorrect!).

Nearly a year has passed and I still haven't received an apology from Zac, who, according to his Instagram account, is far too busy throwing beer bottles at moving cars, punching other skateboarders in the face, taking lots of drugs and spraying his graffiti tag all over the city of Cambridge to do anything as boring as apologise to a middle-aged mum!

A story, then, is an account of what actually happened, containing the necessary context and backstory. It is not a description of your feelings or thoughts about what happened, though it may contain those as well. When I invited people to send me their grudge stories, I received quite a few descriptions of angry and sad feelings that did not tell me what events had caused those feelings.

2. Don't read through your grudge story immediately after you've written it. Leave it alone overnight. (You can do each stage of the method for one grudge at a time, or for a bunch of grudges together – whatever you'd prefer.)

3. The next morning (or at least one full night's sleep later), read through what you've written. What kind of story is it? Is it a story of cruelty or injustice? Neglect? Abandonment? Whatever kind of story it is, see if there is any space anywhere to add some humour. I added humour to my Zac Rawse grudge story by deliberately contrasting Zac's fictitious guilt and contrition as described by his mother with the reality of him sending me abusive messages via my son. When I wrote, 'I started to doubt the sincerity of his contrition . . .', that was a joke – the humour in it being that there was no doubt at all in my mind at that point that Zac Rawse was a conscienceless little arsehole.

Adding humour wherever possible immediately injects a little fun into your grudge story, and if you're having or creating fun, you're creating positive energy, which can take the edge off negative feelings and the desire to wreak a terrible revenge. Whenever I found myself fantasising about spray-painting 'Fucking arsehole' across the front of Zac Rawse's house, I would think to myself, 'Actually, "Ducking arsehole" would be better', and soon I'd be laughing and remembering that taking the mickey out of the crappest master criminal I've ever come across – a boy who gets caught by his friend's mum and ticked off by his own mum before his scam has made him a penny of profit, and who posts evidence of his other crimes all over Instagram for everyone to see and possibly arrest him for later – is a far healthier and more enlightened way of spending my time than becoming a graffiti vandal myself and causing harm to parents who are already unfortunate enough to have Zac Rawse as their son.

4. Once you've added all the humour and fun that it's possible to add to your grudge story (and please don't worry if this turns out to be none at all because you're too devastated by the grudge-sparking incident), read your story again and ask yourself: 'If I could rewrite this story changing only my own actions (because we cannot change our grudgee's behaviour; we are generally powerless to change the behaviour of others, and we need to recognise that or else we'll waste lots of energy), what would I change? In my Zac Rawse grudge story, I would change the part where I cared about trying to spare him a criminal record. I would change the part where, instead of going straight to the police, I contacted his mother and, by doing so, put myself in the position of having to read emails from her in which she told me that Zac had sworn to her (not *at* her – he saved that for me) that his crime had been a complete accident, and that she was inclined to believe him because, really, he was *such* a lovely, honest boy.

5. Now rewrite the story, changing those of your actions that you wish you could change, and adding the different results your altered actions would yield (you get to make this bit up – you're telling a fictional version of the story now, so it's completely up to you). I would end my fictional version of the Zac Rawse story with Zac getting a visit from two stern police officers informing him that the Crown Prosecution Service were going to be taking this further – perhaps as far as a little bit of community service or a fortnight in a Young Offender Institution. Zac would then realise he'd been

a very silly boy, resolve never to defraud anyone again and email me to apologise for what he'd done. At which point, satisfied that he was truly sorry, I would drop all charges (assuming that's something one can do in real life in England, and not just something people say in American legal dramas).

6. Put your two stories side by side, or one above the other, and read first one then the other. Be fully aware of how different those two stories are. Ask yourself: is the strength of your negative feelings around this raw grudge partly a result of either a) frustration at being unable to change the past, or b) anger at yourself for having not done the obvious Right Thing(s) To Do (RTTD)? Usually, you'll find the answer to one or both of these questions is 'yes'. Once you understand this, you'll realise that the powerful negative emotions you're experiencing around this grudge are not exclusively the fault of your grudgee. This awareness will help to dismantle your conviction that you must hate your Zac Rawse equivalent for ever, or strike back at him.

7. Understand that you cannot change the past, or other people. If you struggle with this part, and find yourself thinking, 'But what happened to me was unacceptable, so how can I ever accept it?', you can make your struggle go away by reading *Loving What Is* by Byron Katie, which explains brilliantly and clearly why it is pointless to argue with reality. Yes, what Zac Rawse did to my family was completely unacceptable from a moral point of view, and I will always say so. Yet, he did it. I

can't ever change that. And if I decide that I can't accept *that* – the bare, bald fact that it happened – then I'm trying to argue with an unarguable fact, which is the most pointless activity in the world. So, you must accept that your grudge-sparking incident happened. Wishing it hadn't won't help you. You must accept that your grudgee is damaged/dangerous/hypocritical/ a thieving, graffiti-spraying arsehole and that you are highly unlikely to be able to change him, and so you probably shouldn't try. Let him decide to change, if and when he's ready, and do that work himself. Or not – perhaps he will opt to be a morally bankrupt little shit for ever. It's not your problem.

8. Understand the RTTD (Right Thing To Do) Principle. This is possibly the most crucial step in the grudge-processing method, and I want to introduce it by talking about my dog, Brewster. I'm writing this book on my laptop, in the little courtyard garden of my house in Cambridge. Brewster, my lovely Welsh Terrier, is sitting right next to me, stretched out across some sofa cushions, keeping me company. Now, wouldn't it be the daftest, most irrational and most pointless thing in the world if I was *ignoring Brewster's presence entirely* and if instead I was sighing miserably, fuming resentfully and thinking, 'I wish Buttercup, the Boston Terrier that I don't own – and who, in fact, doesn't exist – was here with me now. I can't relax or feel happy because she isn't here'? Wouldn't that be creating misery for myself that's completely avoidable? Internally ranting about the absence of a nonexistent dog, when I've got a gorgeous

real dog right here beside me? Sheer lunacy! But this, folks, is how many of us carry on in relation to RTTDs. The RTTD in our grudge story often no longer exists. Not always, but often. Take my *The Painting in a Haystack* grudge: the RTTD would have been for me not to allow myself to be emotionally blackmailed into looking for and putting up Laura's painting, motivated by fear of reprisals. I can't do that RTTD right now, and won't be able to in the future, because Laura's no longer in my life, and I no longer own her painting. That RTTD, therefore, is as nonexistent as Buttercup the Boston Terrier and I need to stop thinking about it and fretting about it. *This,* then, is my RTTD, my equivalent of Brewster-my-real-dog-who's-here-next-to-me. My present-moment RTTD is: stop thinking and fretting about RTTDs that no longer exist.

Many of us neglect and leave undone our present-moment RTTDs because we're too busy berating ourselves for having failed to do our past RTTDs. We must abandon past RTTDs completely and put them out of our minds. They no longer exist. Once you understand this, you'll be in a position to attend to present-moment RTTDs.

9. Identify Present-Moment RTTDs, and Do Them. Here is my first present-moment RTTD in relation to my Zac Rawse grudge: ring the police and report him now. 'Wait, *what*?' I hear you say. Isn't that a past RTTD, and therefore nonexistent? Not at all. It's a past RTTD that is still a present RTTD. Why? Because I can still do it! I can still ring the police and report that crime, even though I foolishly didn't at the time. If the RTTDs in your grudge story are things you could still do, and should still do, then do them! If there is action you could take to right a wrong in your grudge story, take it – though remember, it must be done with the positive aim of righting a wrong, not motivated by a 'Hah! I'll make him suffer' desire for revenge. With regard to Laura and *The Painting in a Haystack*, I can't do anything in relation to her or her painting, because I no longer have access to either of them, but that doesn't mean there is no present-moment RTTD available to me. There is: I can and should resolve never again to allow myself to be emotionally blackmailed by an unreasonable person who is stuck in a state of emotional childhood. Which brings me to . . .

10. Learn all the available lessons from your grudge story. When we can't change the events, rights and wrongs of a particular grudge story because the RTTD in the story is no longer a viable option, we shouldn't worry at all – because we *always* have available to us the present-moment RTTD of *learning all the lessons* offered by the story. Once we understand that we can extract useful and powerful lessons from our grudge stories (which will then become our good grudges), we won't feel so inclined any more to wish they hadn't happened. My first RTTD in relation to Zac Rawse was 'Inform the police', which I did. My second RTTD was 'Learn all the lessons I can learn from this'. And I did. The lessons were: make sure my

children understand that stealing is something they must never, ever do under any circumstances; teach my children that some people aren't trustworthy, however cool their skateboards look, and therefore, to be on the safe side, don't ever show anyone your PIN number; teach my children that if they commit a crime or offence against someone, they should apologise properly and do all they can to put it right; make sure I don't forget these things too; make sure I'm never as naive about my children as Zac's mother was about him; in future, if someone steals from me, don't try to create an opportunity for that person to avoid punishment, especially if I don't know whether they're likely to appreciate that or not – instead, understand that it's the police's job and not mine to deal with people who break the law; monitor my bank accounts more regularly, so that thieves who might have infiltrated them don't get to spend quite so long helping themselves to my money before I catch them at it; encourage my son to avoid that particular skateboarding park that is full of drug-taking-and-dealing, graffiti-spraying reprobates.

11. Appreciate the opportunity to learn these lessons, and be glad of the gift of your grudge-sparking incident. If Zac Rawse hadn't stolen my money, I wouldn't now have better control over my various credit cards and bank accounts; I wouldn't have a teenage son who fully understands why stealing is so wrong, and the difference between true, good friends and ne'er-do-wells with whom one happens to share a hobby. Most

importantly of all, I wouldn't have learned that I have spent most of my life indulging in inappropriate and counterproductive lenience in relation to badly-behaved people.

Once you start to appreciate all the lessons your grudge has taught you, you will soon find that you are able to think, 'You know what? In some ways, it's good that that happened,' or, at the very least, 'I'm sorry it happened – I wish it hadn't – but I have benefited from the experience in the following ways: I'm stronger now/I'm wiser now.'

12. Beneath your two versions of your grudge story, list the benefits you have accrued as a result of your grudge-sparking incident. List the reasons why you're grateful to have this grudge in your life. If your grudgee has suffered any consequences, good or bad, list those too. Zac Rawse suffered a very uncomfortable ticking-off from his mother and probably also had to find nearly £500 (his mum paid me back the money he'd stolen, and I'm sure she will have made him pay her back). Anyway, I know he went out and got a Saturday job soon afterwards. Cambridge police have his name, address and a list of all the crimes I know he's committed.

Learn how to handle the residual negative emotion. Your grudge is now processed and ready to go in your Grudge Cabinet, to commemorate the grudge-sparking incident that hurt or angered you and the wrong that was done. Once it's in your Cabinet, your grudge will continue to act as a lesson and an inspiration to you, and you will have no need to cling to any anger or pain. If you find you still have some – if there's part of you that's still screaming, 'But I yearn to push him/her off a tall building!' – then it's fine, and perfectly safe, to accept that you have that feeling *as long as you don't act on it.* Your actions towards your grudgee should never be cruel, unjust, illegal or destructive in any way, but if you want to shout 'BASTARD!' in the privacy of your own living room every now and then, please feel free. That can be a joyous thing to do. Eventually, I promise you, you will stop wanting to – the key is allowing your negative feelings to stick around for as long as they seem to want to, and making them welcome. When we welcome and accept our negative emotions, we are effectively pouring kindness and positivity all over them, and they will soon be incentivised to move towards positivity, or else they will disintegrate naturally and vanish. If you are concerned that your negative emotions aren't shifting quickly enough, I strongly recommend Emotional Freedom Therapy (of which Anne Grey is an expert practitioner) and/or listening to Brooke Castillo's Life Coach School podcast.

Congratulations! You now have a processed grudge. If it still feels like a P1 grudge and not P2 or P3, just keep reading the two versions of the story that you've written, keep thinking about the RTTDs that you did in order to process the grudges, and about the ones you no longer need to worry about because they don't exist any more. Keep rereading your lists of lessons learned, improved behaviours and reasons to be grateful that it happened in the first place. I promise you, that grudge will soon slide out of the P1 category into P2 or P3.

Once your grudge is processed and is P2 or P3, take the papers you've written on (print them out, if you wrote them on a computer), fold them slowly and carefully to symbolise a grudge that is now processed and ready to be formally admitted to your collection – remember, this is The Grudge-*fold* Path – and place them in your Cabinet with as much ceremony as you can muster!

Anne Grey likes the Grudge-fold Path's story-telling approach to grudges: 'Making a grudge or painful sparking incident into a story, preferably with humour, is the perfect way to begin the process of distancing yourself, becoming more detached, less attached to outcome, more able to release the past pain and be fully present now. You are no longer lost in and identifying with your emotions to the same extent. You are changing your relationship with your thoughts and emotions. This is a healthy step!'

And now for my favourite 7-carat grudge. I *love* this grudge – it contains so much hilarious absurdity – and remember, once you're laughing hysterically about how absurd something is, it no longer has anywhere near as much power to hurt you.

The Scared Parents
Grudge type: Cowardice Grudge

When I moved to Cambridge in 2010, I sent my children to a lovely school that had an amazing head teacher, Harriet – she was kind, clever, loyal, devoted to all her pupils and her school. She'd created the school herself, starting with only five families and ten children, and it had been hugely successful. When I first visited to look round, there were more than 200 pupils at the school. I told Harriet that my children wouldn't be able to start there straight away because we were still paying fees to our old school, having neglected to give the full term's notice that was required. Harriet immediately said, 'Oh, don't worry about that! Have a term for free!' In my extensive experience of fee-paying schools, that is an offer that is simply never made, and I was blown away by Harriet's generosity. My children started at her school immediately, and loved it there. If I ever had a problem or a concern, Harriet would come round to my house immediately and discuss it with me, and the problem was quickly resolved every time.

My family was not the only one that felt this way about Harriet. She went above and beyond for every single pupil, parent and teacher. Most people who joined the school, families and staff, did so because they were so impressed by her dedication and the amazingly happy and supportive environment she created. I have been into many schools over the years – as a visiting writer, a parent, a prospective parent – and I have never met another school that has that special joyful vibe Harriet's school had.

You'll notice I said 'had', not 'has'. Past tense. What went wrong? Just about everything. The school was so popular that Harriet eventually felt she had no choice but to bring in a financial partner/investor to fund things like new labs and new buildings. A prospective partner came along, keen to invest, and Harriet sought legal advice. I'm not sure whether it was the advice itself that was the problem, or

Harriet's interpretation of it, or whether she was simply a bit too trusting when the investor-partner said, 'Oh, don't worry, we still absolutely want you to run the school!', but whatever it was, Harriet assumed all would be well and that her new business partners would behave honourably.

Within a very short space of time, The Partners (as I will call them henceforth – it's a much more polite name than the one I started with, I promise you) fired Harriet and replaced her with a different head teacher whom none of the parents knew. Harriet disappeared overnight, and wasn't able to communicate with the parents in any way, or to say goodbye to her pupils or to the school she had created, because of legal constraints that were imposed upon her by The Partners, who were now the majority shareholders. Parents and children were distraught. It seemed to us that The Partners either did not understand how vital a role Harriet played in the life of the school and how important she was in creating and sustaining its wonderful ethos, or else they simply didn't care what any of us might think or want.

I organised a meeting for parents and suggested we explain to The Partners how much we all wanted Harriet to be reinstated. Everyone liked this idea. A further meeting was arranged, with The Partners this time, at which I said to them, 'Harriet was the unique selling point of the educational product that all these hundreds of people have bought into. She is the main reason we're all here, willing to give the school our money. *All* of us, without exception, want her to be reinstated, and we are *all* of your customers, not merely the majority. *We are your entire UK customer body.* If there's one thing I know about business, it's that you don't remove from your product the one aspect of it that *all* your customers like best. Right? I'm actually trying to help you here, to make your business as successful as posssible and increase your profits!'

(I'm very good at sucking up to those in charge when I have to, folks. It's a hangover from my people-pleasing-liar days.)

The Partners would not budge. I'm not sure why. It still makes no sense to me. My best guess is: Harriet is a strong character who likes to do things her way, and The Partners simply didn't want to have to negotiate or compromise with her. One of the parents found an article written by a member of The Partners' company about (I'm paraphrasing here) how to carry out a hostile takeover of a school. This article advised that most of the parents would very soon fall into line and support the new regime. Only a handful of parents, said the article, would continue to cut up rough, and the thing to do then was to explain to them that unless they piped down, their children would be asked to leave the school. I'm almost certain that The Partners believed this would happen at Harriet's school, and that soon they would be able to do what they wanted without too much parental resistance.

After the unsuccessful meeting between the parents and The Partners, I organised another get-together for the parents, to strategize. There was coffee, there was tea, there were biscuits and there was a great plan – at least in my head. We'd all read The Partners' 'How to do a School Takeover' article. I said to the assembled parents, 'These guys think they can defeat us because they're assuming only a handful of us will stand up to them properly. All we need to do is stand firm, all of us, and stand together. We agree not to send them our children or our money, *at all*, not even a five-pound note or a tiny child, until they reinstate Harriet. We organise a campaign and publicise the hell out of it. I was willing to pay, out of my own pocket, for a top London PR firm to publicise our plight and our campaign internationally. 'We can win,' I said. 'We only need to stick to our guns. The Partners, in the face of all their fees and customers disappearing, and in the face of the huge reputational damage they will sustain, will soon cave in and give us Harriet back.'

I said this to approximately three hundred people. Guess how many said, 'Yes, great idea, let's do it!'? I'm not sure exactly how many, but it was fewer than twenty. I will always be hugely grateful to those fewer than twenty people and hold a 'GG' (a gratitude grudge – fully explained in Chapter 10) about them. They were brilliant, all seventeen or eighteen of them.

Here are some of the things the other 280 Scared Parents said, altered very slightly for privacy and to highlight the comic absurdity:

'I'm not keeping Jocasta away from school for a protest. She's meant to be learning about ionic bonding in Chemistry next week. She can't miss that. You don't think The Partners will fire the Chemistry teacher too, do you? I'm scared they will.'

'I'd *love* to join in with the protest, which has such a laudable aim – and as you all know, I'm a socialist revolutionary – but I'm scared the new management will pick on Rukia if they know her mum's one of the troublemakers, so I'm afraid I can't risk joining in.'

(At this point, I said, 'Yes, they might fire the Chemistry teacher. They might do anything at all if we don't show them that they can't get away with it. That's why we need to protest, peacefully but firmly.' I also said, 'No child can be picked on if *every* child's parents are part of the protest. That's why the "Let's all do this, as one" part is so important.')

The Scared Parents could not be persuaded. They said:

'My daughter's in Year 11 – what about her GCSEs? I can't take her out of school. I'd be scared that she'd fail her exams, never be able to take them again and end up a heroin addict living under a bridge.'

'Stop being so negative, Sophie. Let's give these new people a chance! Maybe even though The Partners recently told us that they couldn't give less of a toss about our wishes if they tried, they're secretly lovely and amazing and will soon prove that.'

Here's one that really made me chortle. This suggestion was put forward by a group of parents who thought that the plan suggested by the frizzy-haired crime writer was naive and crude: 'There's no point campaigning to have Harriet reinstated, because The Partners have already told us they're not willing to consider that. So why don't we, instead, campaign for something else that they might be more likely to give us, like permission to form a parent committee with real power, that could hold management to account?'

I pointed out that The Partners would deny, also, the request for a parent committee with real power. Power of any sort was the very thing they were unwilling to give us. What they would do, I predicted, was happily agree to the creation of a sham committee and pretend it was real and powerful, while making sure it wasn't. This was exactly what did happen in the end, and when it did, the parents who had hoped it would work were all disappointed and cross. Their crossness kept them far too busy to email me and say, 'You were totally, 100 per cent right.' No one ever emails you to say that, folks. Ever. And everyone who never comes back and says 'You were right all along' deserves a grudge category all to themselves.

Now, I understand all about cowardice. I myself am regularly a coward, though not as much or as often as I used to be. As a former compulsive people-pleaser, I get it, I really do. What irritated the hell out of me on this occasion was: *there was no serious danger of harm to anybody who decided to join in the protest*. None. The worst – the very worst – that would have happened to any of those parents was a disruption to their children's education. And it could have been a really minor one – all over Cambridge there are schools, state-funded and private, that would have been willing to take in those pupils at short notice. How do I know this? Well, shortly after the protest-that-didn't-happen-because-fewer-than-twenty-people-were-on-board, the school started to fall apart. The new head teacher disappeared altogether, or so it seemed. The Partners then appointed a different head teacher, who, in what seemed like no time at all, was sent to prison for trying to have sex with a nonexistent fourteen-year-old boy – the figment of a paedophile-entrapping vigilante group's imagination.

Many parents took their children out of the school almost immediately after The Partners took it over. (I was one of them.) Other parents followed in dribs and drabs. All of those children found new schools. No one became a heroin addict living under a bridge as a result of the disruption.

On the day Harriet was fired, the senior school (Years 7 to 11) had 199 pupils. As I write this, it has only 40, is in dire financial straits, and will possibly even be unable to open its doors for the next school year. The latest disaster to befall the school was the English department teaching students a syllabus that was no longer current, which resulted in the English GCSE students turning up for their exam and finding that they were expected to answer questions on books they hadn't read.

Many children at the school when The Partners took it over had special educational needs. Those children could not easily be moved, because of SEN teacher provision and other practicalities, and their parents are therefore absolved of all grudgeworthiness. They couldn't risk their children being expelled in a hypothetical future purge of rebel families, in case there was nowhere else for them to go that would cater for their needs. For the rest of us, however, the stakes were relatively low; the worst fate that would have befallen our children was a few slightly delayed GCSE exams. The parent body could have stuck together and got Harriet back in position within weeks, before a brilliant school had been ruined. But a lot of the parents were scared. They chose to define 'sticking up for ourselves and protecting our school' as 'causing trouble', and then decided not to do it.

This is one of my most useful and inspiring grudges. It's

made me suspicious of schools and powerful people within them, and determined to stand up and make a fuss about any school-based injustice. Since this day, I have made sure to let my children know that the adults imposing rules on them are people they should respect and obey *only if* those people do not treat them appallingly unfairly. *The Scared Parents* grudge has also given me a ratio to work with that I think is pretty accurate whatever group of people you apply it to. I have, of course, invented a name for it . . .

THE PROPS-TO-FLOPS RATIO

Out of every 300 people, there are likely to be only twenty, at most, that you can truly rely on to be intelligent, loyal, sensible and to know how to behave properly. Once I understood this, it was a huge relief – now, in any large group, I focus on finding my twenty great people and don't bother to have unrealistically high expectations of the rest.

GRADING *THE SCARED PARENTS* GRUDGE:

1. Was the intention of the grudgee **(The Scared Parents)**:

a) definitely or probably bad

b) possibly bad

c) not bad – they were trying to protect themselves and their children (1 point)

2. Did they know they were upsetting or hurting Harriet?

a) Yes, definitely

b) Possibly

c) **Not at all – I'm going to be lenient here. I believe they all honestly thought that the only people who hurt/wronged Harriet were The Partners. The Scared Parents imagined that they were simply doing what was best for their children. They also did not believe *at all* in our power as a group to change things for the better, so therefore they *also* didn't believe that not trying to change things for the better was an active cause of harm. (1 point)**

3. Was the overall situation:

a) **very serious – the school was Harriet's life's work, her creation and she was shattered by the loss of it. She had been on the verge of buying a house, but without a job or business she couldn't afford to do so. Her husband, who also taught at the school but left when Harriet was fired, was also out of a job. Her children had to leave the school they loved and watch their parents suffer severe strain and anguish. (3 points)**

b) quite serious

c) not very serious

4. Was the effect upon Harriet of what they did or said:

a) **very bad – as described above. (3 points)**

b) quite bad

c) not so bad

5. Should or could they have known/done better?

a) Yes

b) **Maybe. They should have, but their fear prevented them from being capable. They should have worked out that the worst-case scenario associated with doing the right thing wasn't that bad, but they were genuinely in the grip of fear. (2 points)**

c) No

6. Did they cause Harriet real harm?

a) **Yes – in a sin-of-omission kind of way. It was what they didn't do, not what they did, that helped to cause the harm. (3 points)**

b) Maybe

c) No

7. Is the 'Grrrr!' factor of this grudge:

a) high. *So* high. Higher than Bob Marley, Pete Tosh and the Wailing Wailers after smoking many, many spliffs. (3 points)

b) medium

c) low

8. Have you held this grudge:

a) for ages – since September 2015 (3 points)

b) for a medium length of time; or, for a short time and you think you'll hold it for a bit longer but not for ever

c) for a short time

My *The Scared Parents* grudge has 19 points so far.

9. Would this incident, alone, be sufficient to make you hold a grudge about this person or people?

a) Yes (so no points deducted)

b) No

10. Would something bad or frightening have happened to your grudgee if they *hadn't* performed the grudge-sparking action?

a) No – here I'm going to be less lenient. Objectively, a move to another school for your child is not frightening but simply 'one of those things that sometimes has to happen' (so no points deducted)

b) Yes

11. Would this grudge be cancelled out/terminated if your grudgee apologised fully and wholeheartedly?

a) No (so no points deducted)

b) Yes

12. Is your grudgee someone who matters to you, and to whom you matter?

a) Yes, massively

b) Yes, quite a lot

c) Not especially – so points stay the same

The Scared Parents grudge ends up with a total of 19 points, making it a 7-carat grudge.

9

Bad and Invalid Grudges

'The growth of his power and fame was matched, in my imagination by the degree of the punishment I would have liked to inflict on him.'

Vladimir Nabokov

Now that we've looked at how to process a grudge, let's make sure you don't waste time processing grudges that are always going to be invalid or bad, no matter what you do to them, or squander precious Grudge Cabinet space on grudges you no longer need or enjoy.

Doctors have a rule: 'First, do no harm'. Grudge-holders should follow exactly the same rule. The Grudge-fold Path's equivalent of the Hippocratic Oath is: *If your grudge is causing harm or distress to you or anyone else, it should either be processed, significantly altered or ditched*. If you are experiencing additional suffering, over and above the hurt caused by the sparking incident, then that grudge is not a good or processed grudge. A good, processed grudge will alleviate suffering, not increase it. And if keeping your grudge means that you are going to punch or snarl at your grudgee, then your grudge is toxic and needs to be either processed or dumped.

The above rule only works, however, if we're using a correct and fair definition of harm. *Talking, writing or joking about your grudge does not constitute harm.* I'm sure, for example, that at least one of the scared parents from my *The Scared Parents* grudge will read this book and think, 'How dare she? She's harmed me by writing this.' No, I haven't. I've expressed my opinion about a situation we were jointly involved in, which I am allowed to do – just as any other parent from that school would be entitled to write and publish their own account: 'I thought that frizzy-haired crime writer was completely unrealistic and unreasonable, trying to boss us all around and make us join her silly protest.' Everyone is allowed to talk and write about their life and experiences, and other people are free to disagree and offer alternative versions. When we do this, we are not harming anybody, according to a fair and non-repressive definition of harm.

Once we're sure our grudges are doing no harm to us or to others, we can feel free to keep each of them for as long as we wish. If our Grudge Cabinet is getting crowded, we can always buy or make another! It's vital, though, that we don't sully our Cabinets with grudges that should never have been put in there in the first place.

What Makes a Grudge Bad or Invalid?

Please don't panic if you are holding some bad or invalid grudges. It could be that you simply need to process them in order to turn them into good, healthy grudges – and, if that's not the case, then understanding why a particular grudge is invalid will probably inspire you to *want* to abandon it instead of feeling forced to.

THE SCRUDGE

(named after Ebenezer Scrooge) A grudge against the way things were in the past, are in the present or might/will be in the future. You can't change either of the first two, and to resent the future before it arrives, when you have no way of knowing how great it might be, creates a lot of negative energy. Also, you don't know for certain what anybody's going to do in the future. To resent a person for something she might never do is both pointless and absurd.

THE SHIELD GRUDGE

You strongly dislike someone for no good reason, or for an unworthy reason. Then they do something minorly annoying, and suddenly you have the perfect excuse. You seize on this convenient obviously-wrong thing they have done, though really it's all about justifying a pre-existing spiteful or dishonourable resentment.

THE TOXIC GRUDGE

Any grudge that, after processing, is harmful or unpleasant to you or others.

NOTE: remember when we looked at how to process grudges, I said that, even after processing and turning your P1 grudge into a P2 or P3, you might be left with some residual negative emotions, which will pass when they are ready? That still applies! Please do not confuse that residual negative emotion that's left behind by a sparking incident with anything toxic. Here is an illustration of the difference between the two:

A Toxic Grudge brews and solidifies negative feelings and spews them forth (in the way that the magic porridge pot from the traditional story spews forth endless porridge). The more you think about the grudge, the more anger, pain and bitterness you start to feel. The grudge feels synonymous with and inextricable from the original wound-cause.

A Good, Processed Grudge coexists alongside some residual negative emotion left behind by the sparking incident, but each time you think about it, it has the effect of decreasing and disarming – even only slightly, or gradually – the hate, resentment and misery you feel about the sparking incident because the grudge is *not* inextricable from the original wound-cause; it is, instead, an instructive or enlightening story about the original wound-cause.

THE ACTION-SUBSTITUTE GRUDGE

When correct and feasible action would remove your grudge, perform the correct action instead of holding the grudge.

The Strong Tea/Weak Coffee Example

'I've got a grudge against Philippa.'

'Oh, really? Why?'

'Because every time I ask her for a drink, she makes me strong tea, even though I vastly prefer weak coffee.'

'Oh, dear. And . . . she knows this?'

'Er . . . well, no, she doesn't. But I mean, she should be able to work it out.'

'You've never told her?'

'No. I pretend to adore the strong tea – to be polite.'

'Then how could she possibly work out that you secretly want weak coffee?'

'Do I look like the sort of person who'd like strong tea? Ugh!'

THE GROUP GRUDGE

Unless every member of a group committed the inciting offence, don't hold a grudge about all members of that group. It wouldn't be fair. That would be an invalid grudge. For example, if a person named Jemima once poked you in the eye, don't hold a grudge against everyone named Jemima. Most of those Jemimas are innocent. A valid group grudge would be one where every single member of the group is equally implicated – for example, I have a grudge about the group 'People who are incapable of giving proper, fulsome praise or thanks'. Even when they love something and think it's brilliant, they are incapable of uttering the words, 'I love it and think it's brilliant.' If you buy them a gift of something they've wanted for years, they peer at it, say, 'Huh!' and then put it down on a table and walk away. My group grudge is therefore valid because every single member of the group, by definition, indulges in the grudgeworthy behaviour.

THE INHERITED GRUDGE

If the only reason you have a grudge is that your parents and grandparents had it before you and therefore it's an accessory sported by everyone in your family, that is not a valid grudge. You need to choose your grudges for yourself. Never allow the older generations of your family to pass them down in a 'We, the Nuneaton Robinsons, want nothing to do with the Birmingham branch of the Robinson family after what they did in 1953' kind of way. Were you even born in 1953? Even if you were, there's a strong chance that an inherited grudge is one that has nothing to do with you, and that has been inappropriately foisted upon you.

THE SCAPEGOAT GRUDGE (INAPPROPRIATE EXTRAPOLATION GRUDGE)

This occurs when you're too scared to have a grudge about the person you ought to have a grudge about, so you pick an innocent person whose behaviour reminds you of the behaviour you're afraid to recognise as unacceptable.

Example
Tammy is scared of Wendy because Wendy's brothers are all gangsters who occasionally administer beatings with baseball bats. Tammy hates to think of herself as a wimp, however, and so when Wendy borrows Tammy's car without asking permission, over and over again, Tammy convinces herself that it's fine and she doesn't mind at all. Then one day, Tammy's mum, Fiona, comes round and, as she's walking up the driveway, she accidentally touches Tammy's car. Tammy explodes with rage and screams at Fiona, 'Never touch my fucking car again! In fact, get out of my life! I never want to see you again!' This is a clear case of a Scapegoat Grudge. (And a Toxic one – because we should never yell at our grudgees, should we, fellow Grudge-fold Path followers?)

Can you think of any other types of grudge that might be invalid or bad? If so, I'd love to hear from you!

Now it's time for my 8-carat grudge, and we're heading to the good ol' US of A . . .

The American Prosecutor
Grudge type: no. 1, Unprovoked Attack Grudge (though an unusual one. As you'll soon see, this grudge is very hard to assign a type to)

I was in Miami for a book festival. So was a prosecutor who had written a true-crime book about a famous murder case. While prosecuting this case, he had argued for the death penalty but hadn't succeeded in securing it, so the convicted murderer had instead been sent to prison for life.

By coincidence, I had read this prosecutor's book – it was one of the true-crime books I read while doing the research for *Did You See Melody?*, my crime novel set in Arizona – and so I had a pretty good idea of what his views on capital punishment might be, though I knew nothing else about him at this point. I'm against capital punishment, for a range of reasons, but I understood that he wasn't. The subject had not come up at this point, but I found myself thinking, as we chatted in a Miami hotel about recent cases he'd prosecuted, 'I bet he finds anti-death-penalty people like me really annoying. I'm not in favour of the death penalty, but I'm not going to disapprove of him – in fact, if I dealt with what he has to deal with (regularly meeting murderers and their victims' relatives), maybe one day, I'd think, "You know what? Maybe executing people is the right idea after all." I don't think I would. I hope I wouldn't. I hope I would always want the law of the land to be more enlightened than I am when I'm in an angry, vengeful mood, and I hope I would always remember that *Twelve Angry Men* is my favourite movie of all time, and why, but you never know; I might not.'

The prosecutor was very charming and interesting. Late one evening, he and I and another author were sitting in the bar, and he raised the topic of capital punishment, saying that he was sure I must be against it, and that, if I were on a jury in a death penalty case, I would never vote for the death penalty. I was a bit annoyed that he was telling me things about myself after knowing me for only two seconds, and I wasn't sure if he meant that I would vote 'Not guilty' when I believed beyond reasonable doubt that the defendant was guilty, simply to spare them the death penalty, or whether he meant that, having voted guilty, I would then vote for prison, not death, if I could. Either way . . . the prosecutor had known me for about forty-eight hours, and all I'd said to him in that time was that I'd really liked his book, so he had no way of knowing what I would or wouldn't do in a courtroom.

He kept pressing the issue, so eventually the other writer and I felt we had no choice but to discuss it. He was in favour of executing murderers, and we were against it. I noticed he used various unfair and sneaky tactics during our discussion. He kept arguing with something I hadn't actually said, and I kept having to say, 'But I've never made that argument. I'm against capital punishment for *different* reasons – what arguments have you got against *those* reasons?', after which he would simply repeat his refutation of the argument I'd never made in the first place. I *hoped* this was him being rhetorically sneaky and manipulative; I couldn't bear the idea that someone responsible for prosecuting so many life-or-death cases was so imprecise in his thinking. (I don't know why I didn't worry about the sneaky, manipulative stuff – maybe I assumed that lawyers have to be a bit tricksy in order to win cases?)

Despite disagreeing with him about capital punishment, I still – foolishly and naively – believed the American prosecutor was a decent-ish guy. Remember, I had read and admired his book about how he had put a dangerous murderer behind bars where he belonged (and boy, did he belong there!), so I was still giving him the benefit of the doubt at this point.

Then he said to me, 'You got kids?' I told him I had. 'Boys? Girls?' he said. I answered him. 'What does your son call you?' he asked me. 'Mom? Mommy?'

'He calls me "Mum",' I said, wondering why he was asking. He asked me more questions about my son, which I answered. This was ridiculously stupid of me, but it never crossed my mind that anyone might do what he subsequently did.

While I and the other writer listened in horror, the prosecutor launched into a story. He didn't warn me, or explain what he was about to do. He just started telling the story – in the present tense, and in a hushed but excited voice, like a movie trailer ('He's walking along the street, on his way home. He hears a noise in the bushes') – of an imaginary violent attack on my son. The story wasn't short. It included dialogue (this, I discovered, was why the prosecutor had wanted to know what my son called me, because he knew that children call out for their mothers when they are in danger), graphic sexual violence, sadism . . . all the terrible things. He cast my son as the victim in this story and he told it in a deliberately expressive, dramatic way, with the clear intention of making me picture, imagine and experience it as if it were really happening.

I could hear the other writer making uncomfortable and disapproving noises beside me, but this did not stop the prosecutor. I couldn't speak or move. I tried to focus on listening so that I could remember the horror of the experience, for the record. (What record? This book, perhaps.)

Finally, the prosecutor reached the hideous end of his

disgusting tale. He grinned at me and said, 'D'you think you'd *still* be against the death penalty if that happened to your son?'

You might be wondering if I chucked a drink in his face. I didn't. My instinct, in the presence of a truly scary person, is to be charming and polite and protect myself. So, politely, I replied. 'If that happened to my son, I would hunt down the person who'd done it and kill them with my bare hands. But I still believe the law should not be as vengeful, violent and bloodthirsty as I'm capable of being when someone hurts my children. You should read the email I sent to my son's school after a teacher tried to tell him off for not going to a sports lesson that I'd said he didn't have to go to. It was savage. I want the law to be *less* savage than me at my worst. So, yes, I'm still against the death penalty. Gosh, is that the time? It's getting late. I think I'll go to bed now. Goodnight.'

In my hotel room, as soon as I'd closed and locked the door, I started to shake violently. Sitting through the prosecutor's story was the closest I have ever come to being on the receiving end of a violent physical attack. I paced up and down my room, cried, thought about dialling 911, felt hot and feverish, then cold and too weak to stand up. It took me about three hours to calm down.

Once I had, I googled the prosecutor, only to discover that there were current and ongoing disciplinary proceedings against him for precisely this sort of thing. He had been reprimanded regularly, it turned out, for inappropriate behaviour in court, including the invention of fictional scenarios that cast female jurors in the role of victim in imaginary crime scenes. Hence the serious disciplinary proceedings.

What he'd inflicted upon me wasn't a one-off; it was his regular m.o. Once I knew this, I thought: 'I should write down as much as I can remember of the awful story he told me', in case one day I ever need to prove to anyone how beyond the pale it was.

To my shock, I found that I could remember hardly any of it. The incident had only happened about four or five hours previously, and I am someone who normally remembers every detail of conversations that happened thirty years ago, especially if they make a big emotional impression on me. The prosecutor's story, however, had pretty much vanished from my mind less than six hours after I'd heard it. I believe my mind found it too unbearable to hang on to and so simply erased it.

If anything, I am a little more opposed to capital punishment than I used to be, knowing that people like the prosecutor – who, frankly, I wouldn't trust to open a jar of anchovies – are involved in sending people to their deaths. Those people might all be monsters; but how can we be sure, if the people sending them to the electric chair are monstrous too, in their own way?

GRADING *THE AMERICAN PROSECUTOR* GRUDGE:

1. Was the intention of the grudgee (**the American prosecutor**):

a) **Probably bad. He might have wanted, for noble reasons, to promote the system of justice that he felt was most just, but all my instincts told me** that, mainly, he wanted to make me suffer. He really seemed to enjoy describing the more unpleasant details of his story. (3 points)

b) possibly bad

c) not bad

2. Did they know they were upsetting or hurting you?

a) Yes, definitely – that was his sole aim. (3 points)

b) Possibly

c) Not at all

3. Was the overall situation:

a) very serious

b) quite serious – putting into a mother's head that particular story, involving her son, could lead to PTSD. I was actually traumatised for a period of some hours. Other people might have been traumatised for longer. (2 points)

c) not very serious

4. Was the effect upon you of what they did or said:

a) very bad

b) quite bad – psychological trauma, plus a sudden conviction that those practising the law might all be evil. If that's true, maybe it's fine for me to break the law whenever I fancy it? This could lead to general lawlessness in the Cambridge area of England, and the American prosecutor will be to blame for that. (2 points)

c) not so bad

5. Should or could they have known/done better?

a) Yes – the prosecutor is a highly intelligent adult, with enough experience of terrible people that he ought to have 'Don't act like a terrible person' right at the top of his to-do list. (3 points)

b) Maybe

c) No

6. Did they cause you real harm?

a) Yes

b) Maybe

c) No. I'm going to be lenient with this one. Though it felt very much like a violent attack on me and my son, it was only a story. (1 point)

7. Is the 'Grrrr!' factor of this grudge:

a) high. It's beyond Grrrr. It's a void filled with horror. (3 points)

b) medium

c) low

8. Have you held this grudge:

a) for ages. I will hold it for ever. He will never apologise, and he will probably keep gleefully sending people to their deaths, not caring sufficiently whether they are guilty or not. (3 points)

b) for a medium length of time; or, for a short time and you think you'll hold it for a bit longer but not for ever

c) for a short time

My *The American Prosecutor* grudge has 20 points so far.

9. Would this incident, alone, be sufficient to make you hold a grudge about this person or people?

a) Yes (so no points deducted)

b) No

10. Would something bad or frightening have happened to your grudgee if they *hadn't* performed the grudge-sparking action?

a) No

b) Yes

11. Would this grudge be cancelled out/terminated if your grudgee apologised fully and wholeheartedly?

a) No (so no points deducted)

b) Yes

12. Is your grudgee someone who matters to you, and to whom you matter?

a) Yes, massively

b) Yes, quite a lot

c) Not especially – so points stay the same

The American Prosecutor grudge ends up with a total of 20 points, making it an 8-carat grudge.

10

The 'Grudget': Managing Your Grudge Budget

'Be as shrewd as snakes and as innocent as doves. Be on your guard.'

Jesus (*Matthew 10.16-17*)

I'm sure that, like me, you've read about celebrities who plant a tree for every transatlantic flight they take. Managing a 'Grudget' (my nickname for a Grudge Budget) is based on similar principles. In this chapter, I'm going to show you how to get on top of your Grudget using three key techniques: offsetting, vetting and forgetting. Once you've processed all your grudges, eliminated the invalid ones and kept only the good ones, it's time to think about the big picture: the balance in your Grudge Cabinet.

The aim of the Grudge-fold Path is for your grudges, overall, to enhance both your life and the world at large. There are three things you can and should do to maximise the positive effects of your grudges.

1. Every time you add a new processed grudge to your Cabinet, look for one that you can discontinue. Is there, perhaps, one that you don't love or need any more? One that no longer feels interesting, instructive or valuable? If there is, then consider if you could maybe abandon and **forget** that grudge. Commit to a regime of regular Grudge Cabinet spring-cleaning. No one benefits from old, stale grudges languishing dully on Grudge Cabinet shelves. Here are some reasons why you might reasonably decide to get rid of a grudge:

   — **you feel the grudgee is truly sorry, and wishes he hadn't done what he did as much as you wish he hadn't done it.**

   — **you're as sure as you can be that there won't be a repeat of the behaviour, so you have no need to be wary of the grudgee.**

   — **you realise that the grudge was based on a flawed premise.**

Example

I had a powerful grudge against a friend for more than a year because she wrote a book, without telling me she was writing a book. I was in the habit of telling her everything, and I assumed she would reciprocate. I only found out about her book, along with the rest of the world, when it was about to be published. For some foolish reason, I decided to interpret her choice not to tell me as a clear sign that my friend didn't care about me – and, worse than that,

that she had not told me about the book specifically in order to upset me later, when I realised I hadn't been let in on the secret. Then, more than a year later, she spontaneously went out of her way to travel to see me when there was absolutely no need to do so. This showed me that my earlier conclusion was completely wrong and that she did and does care about me. She's simply a more secretive person than I am. I now no longer have that grudge in my Cabinet.

— **you no longer find the grudge instructive or enlightening in relation either to the grudgee or to human beings in general.**

The above example of my friend and the book works here too. There was nothing enlightening about my grudge because no one is under an obligation to tell you something they'd rather not tell you, no matter what you've told them. The lesson of my grudge – 'Anyone who doesn't confide in you about their book, when you've told them all about *your* book, isn't a true friend' – was, not to put too fine a point on it, utter bullshit.

— **you no longer find the grudge entertaining or interesting.**

If the prospect of telling a particular grudge story to a close friend makes you yawn and feel that you can't be bothered, then maybe it's time to eject that grudge from your Cabinet because it no longer resonates or inspires you.

— the grudgee does something so wonderful, unconnected to the grudge, that you are no longer able to hold a grudge about them and that effectively cancels out the theme of the grudge.

Imagine you have a grudge about a close friend who didn't invite you to her birthday party, but *did* invite your ex-husband, even knowing that you dislike him, because it was a swimming party and he happened to be an experienced lifeguard. Then, years later, this same friend goes to great trouble and expense to arrange the best surprise party for you ever. You *might* decide to ditch your grudge about her, seeing how much she cares about you.

Is giving second chances a good thing, from a psychotherapy point of view? Helen Acton says, 'Without Sophie's openness to giving people a second chance, a seasoned collector of grudges could be in danger of what the existentialists would call "objectifying" people – treating them as if they were fixed, unchangeable objects, and not human beings with the potential to surprise us. If we become too rigid with our "I must be wary of Michael, he's the sort of person who . . ." approach to life, then we deny Michael the possibility of changing his behaviour, certainly in specific relation to us, and even increase the chances that we wouldn't spot the change even if it happened!'

Those are just a few of the scenarios that might lead you to abandon or jettison a grudge.

2. Anyone with a Grudge Cabinet also needs a GG (gratitude grudge) Cabinet. A gratitude grudge is a happy story of a great thing someone did, for you or for others, that you want to make a point of remembering – something with a very positive live relevance charge and a wholly benign sparking incident. **Offset** each grudge with a GG. (This does not apply in reverse, incidentally. It is perfectly healthy and acceptable to have more GGs than grudges. The balance should always tip in favour of GGs.)

FIVE OF THE GRATITUDE GRUDGES IN MY GG CABINET:

— When I was on a book tour in South Africa, my laptop got stolen. I was very upset about this, particularly when I learned that my insurance policy didn't cover it. Out of the blue, my South African publisher turned up with a surprise present: a brand new laptop that he'd bought me – the exact same model! Thank you, Eugene!

— Harriet, the wonderful head teacher from *The Scared Parents* grudge story, let my two children have a free term's education at her amazing school. Thank you, Harriet!

— My website designer, Faith, completely of her own volition, spent hours of her time helping me with marketing and telling me everything she thought I needed to know about the business side of being an author, and has completely transformed the way I look at my working life. Thank you, Faith!

— Lucy Cavendish College in Cambridge awarded me
an honorary fellowship and, for the past nine years,
has provided me with the best possible writing room
in Cambridge, with beautiful gardens to look at
while I write. Thank you, Lucy Cavendish!

— Sarah Cowen and Annette Armitage worked with me
on the writing and staging of my first ever musical,
which was one of the best experiences I've ever had.
Thank you, Sarah and Annette!

Add a GG to your GG Cabinet whenever you can! If you're
ever having a difficult day, it really helps to think about your
gratitude grudge stories. And make sure that's what you call
them. If anyone questions your terminology, explain to them
that it's *not* a contradiction to talk about a gratitude grudge,
because grudges are not negative, horrible things – they're
simply stories with a live relevance charge that you want to
remember and that you find enlightening, improving or
entertaining.

3. Vet potential new grudges. However desirable and
beneficial grudges can be, we shouldn't take them on
automatically, without proper consideration. We don't
have to allow in every potential grudge that presents itself.
We can reject some of the wannabe grudges that apply –
and we should. We should be fussy. Ask yourself: am I
sure this grudge is wholly grudgeworthy, valid and good?
Does it add something new, surprising and lustrous to my
Cabinet that none of my other grudges provides?

What if the Object of Your Grudge Dies, or is Punished?

If your grudgee dies, or gets fired or sent to prison for the behaviour that occasioned your grudge against them, does that automatically mean that you'll need to adjust your Grudget to reflect a grudge that's left your Cabinet? Not necessarily. The death or absence of your grudgee might not affect your wish to continue holding the grudge at all, and that's fine. You're not obliged to forget a grudge about a person who has passed away, though most of us would probably want to create some more GGs about that person too. Sometimes a new grudge (often a Selfie Grudge) is created once someone has died. It might take the form of an unresolved feeling: *If only I'd spoken up at the time. If only I'd told them why I was angry and had it out with them while I could.*

There are many valid reasons for not telling people that they have hurt or angered us. Is it always wise to speak up and tell your grudgee about your grudge? Is going public with your grudge always, or even usually, the right thing to do? I would say that there are no firm rules here. One of my grudgees once said to me, 'Is everything okay between us? Because I think I've always been a loving and loyal and great friend to you.' I agreed that she had, and told her everything was fine, even though she hadn't, it wasn't and I was scared even to be in the same room as her. I was convinced (perhaps wrongly – who knows?) that she would be incapable of hearing the truth without lashing out, which would risk causing open and irresolvable conflict between us, something I was not prepared to enter into because I was sure she wouldn't fight fair, and, in any case, I didn't want any sort of fight.

One of my most significant grudges is about someone who told me every single thing they didn't think was ideal about me and every aspect of my behaviour, for most of my life. They felt free to relate to me as if I were their pet creative project, and constantly said, 'You should be more like this, less like that, do more of the other, a bit less of that thing over there . . .' On and on it went. Perhaps it's not surprising, then, that I err on the side of *not* raising for discussion the grudgeworthy things that my grudgees have done.

If your grudgee is punished, either legally or karmically, for their grudgeworthy behaviour, you might find that your grudge about them starts to dissolve. Or, you might find that its live relevance charge remains as strong as ever. Follow your instincts. You will know, better than anyone else, if your grudge is a keeper or a has-been.

And now for my 9-carat grudge. I found this story quite implausible while it was happening, but I promise you, it really did happen . . .

The Ignoring of the Big News
Grudge type: no. 19, Rudeness Grudge

In 2012, I bought a holiday home in the Cotswolds, the house that features in 'Boundary Violation Grudge' in Chapter 3. Most people who knew me knew that my husband and I lived in the centre of a city, had been looking for a rural retreat for ages and were growing rather dispirited because it seemed impossible to find anywhere suitable. Then, suddenly, we found a small cottage that was ideal for our purposes, made an offer and had it accepted. Shortly afterwards, two people we were extremely close to came round for dinner (let's call them Flora and Carl).

We told them our exciting news. I presented it in a 'Ta-da! We have something to tell you!' kind of way, so they knew how excited I was. Flora responded as I'd expected her to, and as almost anyone would: 'Ooh, that's amazing! Have you got pictures?' Carl said nothing. From the moment he heard the words, 'We've bought a holiday place!', his behaviour changed drastically. Without leaving the room, he completely removed himself from the conversation. He looked away, picked up a newspaper and started very ostentatiously to leaf through it, sending a clear message that he wasn't going to participate in this particular discussion.

Though I continued to try to include Carl by making sure to look at him as well as Flora as I answered her questions about the house and showed her pictures of it, he didn't meet my eye again for the entire time that the house was the topic of conversation. Instead, he stared at the newspaper, and, over my head, he half-whispered, half-hissed questions to my children, who were sitting on the other side of the room, behind me: 'How's school?' to my daughter, and 'Did you watch the football on Saturday?' to my son.

Flora, my husband and I were all acutely aware of Carl's odd behaviour. The instant the subject changed from my newly bought house to something else, he joined himself back in and chatted normally to us all, as if nothing had ever been amiss. Flora later asked him why he had behaved so strangely, and he denied that he had. When she described his behaviour to him, he flat-out denied it and claimed he had joined in and showed an interest.

I should point something out, in case anyone imagines Carl might have been envious because perhaps he too wanted to buy a holiday home but couldn't afford it. That was far from being the case. Carl was a wealthy man. He could have bought an extremely snazzy holiday home himself if he had wished to. Why, then, did he respond with such obvious rudeness to my news?

After the event, I speculated about this at length with my husband and with Flora. Here are a few theories:

1. Carl's need for control of my husband and me had been thwarted. He would have liked us to consult him before making such a major decision, not present him with a fait accompli.

2. Carl's feeling were hurt. He had always wanted, and told himself that he had, a closer friendship with us than we had ever wanted with him. He therefore would have expected to be told we were considering buying a house, and maybe even asked to come and look at any house we were thinking of buying.

3. Carl disapproved of the way my husband and I lived our lives in general – he believed we were too impulsive, and therefore hated the 'saw it, loved it, bought it then and there' aspect of our news, which I totally led with. I have always been optimistic and spontaneous, whereas Carl is a worrier and an envisager of worst-case scenarios.

4. Carl was annoyed because he fundamentally wasn't interested in houses – mine, his or anyone's – and so he resented the fact that the conversation was now going to revolve around a boring old house for at least an hour.

5. Carl was angry to find himself being told at the same time as Flora. He liked to think of himself as more important, so might have wanted to be told first and separately.

The next time I saw Carl, he made sure to ask about the house and to seem very positive about it, but, in my dealings with him forever after, I have found that I cannot and do not want to forget that he chose, on first hearing this news that was an exciting big deal for my husband and me, to react in the way that he did. There are not many truly special days or pieces of exciting news in most of our lives. I think we need to be wary of people who 'just happen to' ruin those occasions for us.

GRADING *THE IGNORING OF THE BIG NEWS* GRUDGE:

1. Was the intention of the grudgee **(Carl)**:

a) definitely or probably bad. It's nasty and rude to shun a conversation about the huge good news of someone you allegedly care about. You couldn't do that and not know you were being a git. (3 points)

b) possibly bad

c) not bad

2. Did they know they were upsetting or hurting you?

a) Yes, definitely – see above answer. I believe Carl was deliberately punishing me by withholding his attention, speech, approval and congratulations. (3 points)

b) Possibly

c) Not at all

3. Was the overall situation:

a) very serious

b) quite serious – one way to look at it is to say, 'Well, nothing bad happened to me as a result, so it can't have been serious.' But when someone behaves callously over something that is particularly special to you, it can seriously damage the relationship. This incident was proof, as far as I was concerned, that Carl didn't have my best interests at heart and was not good for me. (2 points)

c) not very serious

4. Was the effect upon you of what they did or said:

a) very bad

b) quite bad

c) **not so bad – it would have been worse if I hadn't already strongly suspected that Carl believed he had a God-given right to be horrible whenever he felt like it, and learned not to take it personally. (1 point)**

5. Should or could they have known/done better?

a) **Yes. Carl had a responsible, public-facing job for many years. He knows the difference between polite, civilised, caring behaviour and acting like a spoilt, angry child. (3 points)**

b) Maybe

c) No

6. Did they cause you real harm?

a) Yes

b) Maybe

c) **No (1 point)**

7. Is the 'Grrrr!' factor of this grudge:

a) **high. What an absolute knob-end. There's huge 'Grrrr' attached to this kind of petty knob-endery. (3 points)**

b) medium

c) low

8. Have you held this grudge:

a) **for ages. Since 2012. And it's a keeper! (3 points)**

b) for a medium length of time; or, for a short time and you think you'll hold it for a bit longer but not for ever

c) for a short time

For each of your answers to the above questions, award your grudge 3 points for an a) answer, 2 for a b) answer and 1 for a c) answer. You'll then have a number of total points.

My *The Ignoring of the Big News* grudge has 19 points so far.

9. Would this incident, alone, be sufficient to make you hold a grudge about this person or people?

a) **Yes (so no points deducted)**

b) No

10. Would something bad or frightening have happened to your grudgee if they *hadn't* performed the grudge-sparking action?

a) No (so no points deducted)

b) Yes.

11. Would this grudge be cancelled out/terminated if your grudgee apologised fully and wholeheartedly?

a) No. I'd always want to remember that the urge to negate, deny and disown my really exciting good news might surface in Carl again when he was next feeling irritable. (so no points deducted)

b) Yes.

12. Is your grudgee someone who matters to you, and to whom you matter?

a) Yes, massively

b) Yes, quite a lot. A compromise answer. I matter to him massively. He would matter to me massively if he hadn't been dickish to me quite so often and failed to take responsibility for it every time. (2 points)

c) Not especially

The Ignoring of the Big News grudge ends up with a total of 21 points, making it a 9-carat grudge.

11

How to Be A Responsible Grudge-Holder

'It is a man's own mind, not his enemy or foe, that lures him to evil ways.'

Buddah

If you want to become a psychotherapist, one of the key elements of the training is to have therapy yourself. You have first to be treated yourself before you can treat other people. It's easy to understand why: it's important to know from personal experience how it feels to be on the other side of the table, as it were.

The same is true of grudge-holding. That's why anyone who is serious about embarking upon the Grudge-fold Path needs to understand that *every grudge-holder is also a grudgee.* It's just about possible, I suppose, that you are the subject of not one single grudge in someone else's Grudge Cabinet, but it's highly unlikely, unless you were only born a week ago.

We're more likely to be responsible grudge-holders if we think regularly about how it makes us feel to be grudgees. In what circumstances might we yearn to have the grudges about us cancelled out? Is there any positive action we can or should take to try to address any of those true stories in which we are the grudgee?

Here are the steps we need to take:

1. Accept that other people are as entitled and as likely to hold grudges about us as we are to hold grudges about them.

2. Try, wherever possible, to behave in ways that do not cause other people anger or pain that they will create a grudge about. This does not apply to their unreasonable anger caused by our entirely reasonable behaviour, or to the pain they cause to themselves and wrongly attribute to us. For example: **you need to stop** walking up to strangers and saying, 'Yours is the most appalling complexion I've seen in years. Why don't you stay inside, or put a bag over your head before going out?' **You do not need to stop** playing tennis with Annabel on a Friday afternoon if it makes Yvonne sad because she doesn't like Annabel and thinks you should only ever play tennis with her.

3. If, for some reason, you realise you have behaved badly to someone, do what you can to put it right: apologise, buy them a nice scarf or a cocktail, reassure them that you care about them and hate the idea that you've hurt them.

4. Accept that once you've apologised and corrected your bad behaviour, you have done all you can do. If they want to hold a grudge, that's up to them – and that's fine.

5. Accept that it's perfectly okay, and nothing for you to worry about, if, even after your apology or behaviour-correction, that person's grudge about you still exists. You cannot control what other people think or how they feel, and you shouldn't try to.

6. Accept that three, or twenty, or 200 people having grudges about you doesn't make you a bad person. It says precisely nothing about you. If I announced that I was going to vote for a particular political party at the next election, the many thousands of supporters of the other party might then have a grudge about me. That's okay: being a person doing her stuff in the world is going to cause people to cast you in a leading role in some of their grudges. It's unavoidable. Do not sit at home doing and saying nothing in the hope of annoying and upsetting no one. People will *still* have grudges about you – 'That stupid sap who hides in her house all day, she's so depressing to live next door to. I have a grudge about her for not moving somewhere else where I don't need to look at her scared, miserable face' – so you might as well enjoy yourself and do your thing in the world to the fullest (responsible) extent.

If I were to decide to start teaching The Grudge-fold Path formally, with lessons and certificates and all that hoo-ha, I would insist that all trainees make a list of grudges they can think of that belong to other people, in which *they* are the grudgee. Here are four of mine:

Grudges People Hold About Me, and My Grudge Accounting Around Them:

1. *Taxi for Dr Interesting Surname*

A former boss of mine thought I was a terrible employee. She still holds a grudge about this, and I keep hearing from people that she encourages people not to read my books. She is also annoyed that I used her surname for a minor character, and thinks I did this to annoy her.

I didn't use her name to annoy her; I used it because it's a great name, and really unusual. I just loved the name! I was a pretty terrible employee when I worked for a different boss in the same institution, before this particular boss took over. Eighty per cent of the reason I was terrible at my job was my fault: I hadn't ever wanted the job, and had agreed to take it on as a favour to a friend who flat-out lied to me. He said, 'It's really part-time, you'll only have to come in one day a month at most.' When I accepted the job, I discovered that the then-boss expected me to be in for approximately half of every week, which was neither feasible nor desirable for me. At the same time as I was hired, another new employee was also taken on and immediately given lots of special treatment and exemptions; she, for example, was *not* expected to come in for half of each week, and I was supposed to accept this and feel okay about it.

Instead of instantly resigning, I stayed and did the job lazily and resentfully for several years. That was my fault. Knowing I couldn't and didn't want to do the work wholeheartedly, I should have left. I stayed in bad faith. Then my old boss moved on and a new boss started – the one with the interesting surname. She had never told me that another employee was far more important than me when we were doing the exact same job, nor had she insisted I come in for half of each week when there was absolutely no reason for me to do so, nor had she once said to me in the most patronising tone imaginable, 'You're a brave girl!', after I'd asked a visitor to our workplace an intelligent and challenging question, as my old boss had. Interesting Surname Boss was absolutely fine, and I had nothing against her. I tried to be a bit better at the job and more conscientious. It worked. I became a more dutiful and well-behaved employee.

During the reign of Interesting Surname Boss, I had my second maternity leave. Some way into it, a colleague rang me and begged me to come back early. There was a particular task that needed doing that he knew I would do happily and easily – it was my favourite part of the job – and that he would have hated to have to do. I agreed to interrupt my maternity leave to do this task, on the condition that I wasn't expected to do anything else. He and I had a meeting with Interesting Surname Boss and she agreed quite readily.

I did the task. Some weeks later, I received an unfriendly email with a distinctly authoritarian tone from Interesting Surname Boss, admonishing me for having neglected to do another task that had been assigned to me. I emailed to say, 'Remember, I'm still on maternity leave, and only agreed to interrupt my leave to do that other thing?' Interesting Surname Boss did not remember. She told me that she had no memory of the conversation at all, and gave me the distinct impression that she believed I was lying.

Luckily, my colleague who had been present for our meeting was able to back me up.

Interesting Surname Boss was most ungracious about this. She neither apologised nor fully conceded she had made a mistake. She said only that she had no choice but to accept this version of events if my colleague and I were both going to insist on saying that was what happened. I am sure she holds a grudge to this day about The Task She Assigned To Me That I Negligently Failed To Perform.

That's fine by me. If she wants to think the worst about that incident, and about me as a result, I'm happy for her to do so. If she wants to tell herself I used her surname in a book to annoy her, I'm happy for her to do that too. I don't feel I need to take any action about this grudge of which I am the grudgee. I, of course, have my own grudge about the same incident, of which Interesting Surname Boss is the grudgee, and from which the lesson I have learned is: try not to end up believing someone is in the wrong and lying when they aren't. If it's possible and plausible that the opposite is true, then try to believe that it is, especially when all that's preventing you is your pride. Believing the worst about someone's motives and behaviour when you have the option not to do so releases corrosive energies that might end up harming the believer.

After Interesting Surname Boss's ungraciousness, I swiftly became a Bad Employee again. I wasn't allowed to park my car in the courtyard right outside our building's front door. No one was. There was a barrier that was only lifted for taxis that would not be staying long. After The Maternity Leave

Mix-Up, whenever I drove to work, I would drive right up to that barrier and say into the intercom, 'Taxi for Dr Interesting Surname', and the barrier would lift. I'd drive in and park outside the building's front door all day. I was eventually caught, but – astonishingly – not until my last ever day in the office. I do wonder if, as a result of believing the worst, Interesting Surname Boss now experiences delays when she orders taxis because the barrier-lifting staff are more suspicious.

Do I need to take any further action in relation to this grudge in which I am the grudgee? No. I only need to remember the lessons: don't believe the worst when you can believe the best, and don't accept or stay in a job you never wanted to do in the first place. If you take on a job, do it wholeheartedly and to the best of your abilities. Part of the reason Dr Interesting Surname thought the worst of me was that my original boss at that firm told her I was a lazy waste of space – and that was wholly my fault, because I *was* lazy and unconscientious.

2. *Never Ringing Norma*

Norma, who lives in Toronto, very much wanted to speak to me on the telephone. She tried my landline twice, but both times I was out. So she sent a message via a third party, Olive, asking if I would ring her. Olive said to me, 'You must ring Norma – she really wants to speak to you.' I didn't want to speak to Norma at the time. Two days earlier, a very short but very traumatic period of my life had ended, and this trauma had affected Norma too – in fact, that was what she wanted to talk to me about; but I didn't want to have the conversation. I thought to myself, 'Maybe later, but not now, when the traumatic episode is so recent.'

I didn't ring Norma. Olive kept nagging me to do so, and I kept saying 'Hmm' non-committally, but I knew I wasn't going to. Instead, I sent Norma a really nice card in the post, making it clear that I was sending lots of love and hoped all was as well as could be expected with her, and being very warm and friendly. My card, which was accompanied by a present, could have left Norma in no doubt that my failure to ring her was nothing to do with any ill-will on my part. Olive, however, disapproved hugely of my not ringing Norma. It did not occur to Olive that Norma's desire to have a telephone conversation with me didn't necessarily mean that I therefore had a duty to ring her. Olive told me that she thought it was 'disgraceful' that I had not rung Norma. I think she still believes this, to this day, and has a grudge about my letting-down of Norma.

Do I need to take any action about this grudge? No. I am happy with the way I behaved in relation to Norma. If I'd been feeling stronger, I might have put her needs ahead of mine, but I wasn't, and I simply felt incapable of speaking to her at that moment in my life. I could try to explain this to Olive, but here's why there would be no point: Olive is a people-pleaser. It's amazing that she managed to tell me that my not ringing Norma was disgraceful, in fact; I suspect it's the only time in her adult life that she's openly criticised someone. If I tried to explain to Olive why I behaved as I did, she would undoubtedly say, 'Oh, of course, yes, I quite understand, yes, you're absolutely right,' and I would have no way of knowing if her grudge about my allegedly disgraceful behaviour was still present in her Grudge Cabinet or not. Therefore: there is no useful action I can perform in relation to this grudge.

3. *Being Insensitive to Simon*

When I broke up with my boyfriend Simon in order to go out with Chris, whom I fancied more, Simon was devastated. A few months later (after splitting up with Chris, who turned out to be very strange indeed), I met Simon in a local pub. He clearly hadn't got over our break-up, and I decided to try and compete with him in the unhappiness stakes. I told him in great detail about how badly Chris had treated me, which was deeply insensitive of me. I think I probably felt guilty and wanted to show Simon that I too had suffered, but it was not okay for me to do that after the pain I'd put him through. A useful action I can perform now is apologising. I'm sorry, Simon. I've searched and searched online for you so that I can apologise to you properly, but you share a surname with billions of people, so I can't find you.

4. *The Bellowing in the Kitchen*

Seth was standing in my kitchen, bellowing at me.

'If I shot someone in the head right in front of you, and then told you I *hadn't* just shot that person dead, what would you say?' he raged. 'Would you say, "Oh, okay then, I suppose we all have different perspectives on the situation", or would you say, "You're a *fucking liar,* I just saw you shoot and kill him"?' This was *not* the situation Seth was bellowing about while I cooked him dinner in my kitchen. Nor did it even really resemble the situation.

My husband, who'd been working upstairs and had been interrupted by the bellowing, at that point appeared in the hall outside the kitchen door. Seth noticed him there, stopped yelling at me, smiled at my husband and, in a friendly, light tone, said, 'Oh, hi, Dan! Sorry, I'll come and chat to you in a minute.'

Dan was clearly nonplussed by this sudden switch and wandered off back to his study. Once he was out of the way, Seth started furiously laying into me again. He had a grudge about me, you see.

Seth had a girlfriend called Trixie. A few weeks earlier, he had told me that he planned to issue Trixie with an ultimatum. Seth and Trixie had an acquaintance called Rafiq who had once been a close friend of Seth's . . . until Rafiq had disagreed with Seth about events that, many years earlier, the three of them (Seth, Trixie and Rafiq) had been jointly involved in.

Seth thought Rafiq's version of events was a flat-out lie. Rafiq, meanwhile, believed that Seth and others (not including Trixie) had behaved unjustly towards him in a way that had caused him harm. Unwilling to accept what he saw as a false and slanderous version of past events, Seth cut off Rafiq altogether.

For a few years, this cutting-off was enough for Seth. Then it started to bother him that Trixie had not also taken action in relation to Rafiq and hadn't cut him off.

At this point Seth told me, having requested 'an important meeting', that he planned to issue his ultimatum: either Trixie must tell Rafiq that she agreed with Seth and ask him to recant his version of past events because it was a lie, or else Seth would regard her as a disloyal betrayer, and very probably end their relationship.

I said, 'Seth, I support you in the sense that I want you to be happy, and not bring unnecessary misery into your life. I think it's okay, sometimes, that people don't agree with us about other people, and whether to keep those people in their lives or not, and I don't think it's reasonable for you to insist that Trixie must demonstrate her "loyalty" to you by doing anything in relation to Rafiq that she hasn't already done of her own volition. She thinks Rafiq is wrong about the past events, but she also accepts that the situation might have looked very different to him from the way it looked to you and her. And that's okay. That's not her betraying you.'

Seth shut down completely. His eyes lost their warmth, he stiffened and his mouth became small and tight. Imagine how someone would behave if forced to sit across a table from someone who, a week earlier, had stolen their life savings or tried to set fire to their pet rabbit; that was how Seth behaved, as soon he saw that I wasn't going to greenlight his threatening of Trixie as enthusiastically as he hoped I would.

I tried to talk him round, but Seth continued to be cold and disapproving and we said goodbye soon afterwards.

The next day, another of Seth's friends rang me and asked if I could please ring Seth, because he was very upset about the way I'd behaved. I don't know why he wanted me to ring him rather than just ringing me himself, but I did so.

Seth seemed pleased at first, but then grew angrier than ever when he realised that I was not ringing to apologise and say that I'd seen sense and now agreed with his ultimatum plan. I'm sure Seth at this point formed a grudge about my treachery and collusion with the dishonest forces of darkness, if he hadn't already done so the first time I gave him my view of the matter.

He ignored my advice, and delivered his ultimatum to Trixie. Wanting to pacify him and please him, Trixie agreed to write a letter to Rafiq. Seth brought it round and showed it to me on the night of the *Bellowing*. It went into great detail about the past events and ended with words to the effect, 'I know that your understanding of the truth is different from mine, and I regret very much that this is the case, but I suppose the same events can look very different to different people.'

Seth asked me what I thought of the letter and I said, 'I think you should be pleased. She took action when you asked her to, demonstrating that she cares about you. And she unambiguously states in this letter what she believes to have happened, which corresponds in every detail with your version of events.'

This was when Seth started to bellow at me. At one point he bellowed that I was probably the sort of person who would deny that a person who'd been shot dead had been shot dead.

I so regret that I continued to try to persuade Seth to be reasonable, that I still made and served him dinner and remained friendly and polite to him all evening even though he had bellowed at me and then sulked for the rest of the night. I deeply regret that at regular intervals throughout my life, I have allowed myself to be not only bellowed at in my kitchen but also sworn and raged at in my lounge, insulted in my hall, psychologically intimidated in my utility room, bullied in my daughter's bedroom and sneered at in my back garden.

If I had my time again, I would say, on all of those occasions, 'If you can't speak to me politely and respectfully, I'm going to have to ask you to leave.' Well, I might. Maybe I'd still be too much of a people-pleaser to follow through. I'd love to be able to put this to the test. I would love it if Seth could come round and rant furiously at me in my conservatory. Sadly, this is impossible. Seth passed away a few years ago, and also I don't have a conservatory.

Seth's grudge about me 'disloyally letting him down' over the Trixie/Rafiq issue is not one on which I am able to take further action. If Seth were still alive, I would certainly not wish to apologise to him, and I would not attempt to discuss the matter with him again unless and until I saw signs from him that he was willing, finally, to consider the possibility that someone who sees things differently from him is not necessarily an enemy.

My *The Bellowing in the Kitchen* grudge out-grudges Seth's *Sophie Not Agreeing With Me* grudge. I hold a more powerful grudge about his behaviour than he did about mine, I think. It was a tense grudge stand-off, from the day that Seth bellowed at me in my kitchen until the day he died, leaving my grudge stranded, with no grudge opponent to square up to.

Before you can call yourself a responsible grudge-holder, you need to go through the process of listing all the grudges you can think of in which you are the grudgee, and assess whether there's anything you can or should do or say, assuming you agree that you wrongfully caused someone else harm. If there is, then do that thing! If there isn't – if you think the grudge-holder is being unfair, or is mistaken – then no action on your part is needed.

For each of your 'I, Grudgee' stories, ask yourself: was the grudge-holder right to be offended or hurt by what you did? Why did you do it? Would you do it again? How might you set things right now, and would you be willing to try? Would you be willing to accept rejection? Willingness to accept rejection of our apologies by those we have wronged is crucial – to our own peace of mind and because to try to force someone to accept your apology constitutes a new grudge-worthy incident.

Once you have done your 'I, Grudgee' inventory and question-answering exercise, you can turn your attention once more to the grudges of which you are the holder . . .

Responsible Grudge-Holding: The Rules

1. No further harm to you or anyone else should result from your grudge.

2. The aim of your grudge should always be to reduce harm and increase justice, wisdom and satisfaction in yourself and in the world.

3. Revenge fantasies are fine, but actual revenge is never justified.

4. Shouting 'That absolute wanker!' in the privacy of your own home in order to entertain yourself and let off steam is fine; shouting it so that your grudgee might hear it, or hear about it afterwards, is not okay.

5. Every so often, let each of your grudges 'appeal' to leave the Cabinet and be discontinued.

Our grudges represent a vital part of our emotional history. They are some of the stories that, together, make up our entire life story. We should honour these stories, and the lessons learned from them, that played a role in making us the people we are today.

Helen Acton says: 'For Jean-Paul Sartre, existential philosopher and influencer of present-day existential therapy, our job as human beings is to uncover and clarify our "fundamental project", which could be described as the unifying basis on which we make our choices and make distinctive the shape of our individual lives. We could say that Sophie's Grudge Cabinet, coupled well with empathy, is a means to that end. It allows her to see, grudge by grudge, what unifies her beliefs about herself and her world, and crucially, determines her choices about her own way of being in the world. Part of Sophie's fundamental project is to be welcoming to those loved by those she loves, and this grudge helps remind her of her plan to live in that way. It affirms her self-construct – the sort of person she wants to be.'

We all have negative, unworthy, dishonourable and destructive feelings and thoughts. We all feel anger and pain, and we gain nothing, and cause further problems, by trying to gloss over or sugar-coat the negative impulses within us. Our Grudge Cabinets, responsibly maintained according to the tenets of the Grudge-fold Path, allow us to keep the majority of our lives and relationships positive. Those of you who still believe that you should hold no grudges, please turn back to the beginning and read this book again.

Now that I've explained in detail how to hold great grudges for a happier life, I'd like to share with you the whopping 10-carat grudge that I've been saving up for last . . .

The Death Wish on the Doorstep
Grudge type: no. 18, Injustice Grudge

My sixteen-year-old niece Tanya (whom I adore) was dating a boy, Jordan. She was very much in love with him and he felt the same way about her. They were at the same school, and had been together for seven months, but she'd never been invited to his house, and whenever one of his parents phoned him when he was with Tanya, he left the room to take the call. Tanya had wondered if perhaps Jordan was keeping some aspect of his home life a secret, and she'd asked him about it many times, but he'd assured her that there was no secrecy involved. He told her that his parents knew all about her and approved of the relationship.

Then one day, Tanya and Jordan were at Tanya's house and the doorbell rang. Tanya's mum answered the front door and found a man and a woman on the doorstep. Their clothing clearly indicated to Tanya's mother that they were members of a religious organisation that required people to dress in a particular way. Sure enough, as soon as the door was open, Jordan's mum told Tanya's mum that they were proud members of a religious group – one that Tanya's mum had heard of and regarded as dangerous and repressive.

Jordan's mother started shouting aggressively that, in their group, no boyfriend–girlfriend activity was allowed at all, and no relationship of any sort was permitted between a group member and someone from outside the group – not even friendship. Tanya and Jordan appeared at this point, having heard the shouting, and Jordan's mother shouted at Tanya, 'Don't ruin my son's life!' Tanya's mother tried to explain to Jordan's that the two teenagers were in love and ought to be allowed to pursue their relationship if they both wanted to. Hearing this made Jordan's mother almost hysterical. She turned to Jordan and screamed at him, 'I hate you, Jordan! I'd be happy if you were dead rather than in a relationship with this girl!' When she shouted these words, neither Jordan nor his father looked surprised – it was clearly not regarded in their family as an unacceptable thing for her to think or say.

Jordan did not have the courage to stand up to the mother who loudly wished death upon him on a stranger's doorstep, and so Tanya had no choice but to accept that her relationship, which otherwise might have lasted, was over. She forgave Jordan instantly for lying to her, understanding that he had only done so because he'd been desperate to pretend to the world and to himself that he had the freedom other teenagers have to choose their own friends and romantic partners.

Jordan and Tanya still secretly text each other for hours every day, and they're still in love – but they can never be officially and openly a couple, because Jordan's parents care more about the rules of their group than they care about their son's freedom or happiness.

GRADING *THE DEATH WISH ON THE DOORSTEP* GRUDGE:

1. Was the intention of the grudgee **(Jordan's parents)**:

a) definitely bad. They intended to forcibly end a relationship that made Jordan very happy, and deny him the basic human right of liberty. (3 points)

b) possibly bad.

c) not bad

2. Did they know they were upsetting or hurting **Jordan**, or being unfair?

a) yes, definitely – and they didn't care. Their group's rules mattered more to them (3 points)

b) possibly

c) not at all

3. Was the overall situation:

a) very serious. Exercising coercion in order to kill a loving relationship is an abuse of basic human rights and human decency. (3 points)

b) quite serious.

c) not very serious

4. Was the effect upon **Tanya and Jordan** of what they did or said:

a) very bad, in an 'opportunity cost' kind of way. What if Tanya and Jordan could have lived happily together for ever, got married, had children? What if Jordan's parents deprived the couple of years of future happiness? (3 points)

b) quite bad.

c) not bad

5. Should or could they have known/done better?

a) yes (3 points)

b) maybe

c) no

6. Did they cause real harm?

a) yes – trying to oppress someone and deprive them of basic freedoms is right up there with the worst harms one person can do to another. (3 points)

b) maybe

c) no

7. Is the 'Grrrr!' factor of this grudge:

a) high. Higher than high, in fact. Think Sid Vicious at his most heroin-infused, then add Jim Morrison at his most substance-abusing, and even *then* you won't be imagining anything as high as the Grrrr factor of this grudge. (3 points)

b) medium

c) low

8. Have you held this grudge:

a) I will hold this grudge for ever and take it into the afterlife with me too. (3 points)

b) for a medium length of time; or, for a short time and you think you'll hold it for a bit longer but not for ever

c) for a short time

My *The Death Wish on the Doorstep* grudge has 24 points so far.

9. Would this incident, alone, be sufficient to make you hold a grudge about this person or people:

a) yes (so no points deducted)

b) no

10. Would something bad or frightening have happened to your grudgee if they *hadn't* performed the grudge-sparking action?

a) no

b) yes – in their eyes, God would have judged and maybe punished them and Tanya if the relationship had continued. (So minus 1 point.)

11. Would this grudge be cancelled out/terminated if your grudgee apologised fully and wholeheartedly?

a) no

b) yes – if they saw the light, left the group and if it wasn't too late for Tanya and Jordan . . . (so 1 point deducted)

12. Is your grudgee someone who matters to you, and to whom you matter?

a) Jordan's parents matter massively to Jordan – so much that their emotional blackmail and death wishes on doorsteps are enough to make him give up a girl he loves and a relationship that made him really happy. (Add 4 points)

b) yes, quite a lot.

c) not especially

The Death Wish on the Doorstep grudge ends up with a total of 26 points, making it a 10-carat grudge.

12

Other People's Grudges

'You are not worth another word, else I'd call you knave.'
William Shakespeare, from "All's Well That Ends Well"

Now let's have a look at some of your grudges – ones that you have been kind enough to send me for this book. I received hundreds, and sadly couldn't include them all, but here is a selection of my favourites:

'I queued for hours in the rain to see the new James Bond movie. When I finally reached the ticket desk, I was told that all the tickets had sold out. I have borne a grudge against James Bond movies since that day, and have never again attempted to watch one.'

'After nearly seven years, I still hate my biology teacher after she (incorrectly) "corrected" me on twins' fingerprints. She insisted they were identical fingerprints. This is impossible! Screw you, Mrs [name redacted].'

'My dad was once woken too early for his liking by a Salvation Army brass band. He held a grudge against the Salvation Army for decades, possibly even until he died.'

'As a children's author, I have a huge grudge against The Gruffalo (aka "The Sodding Gruffalo") – not the author or the illustrator, just The Sodding Gruffalo. He has terrible teeth, terrible claws and a terrible effect on all other children's picture-book sales.'

'Many years ago there was a rather wimpy young man who visited our place of work regularly. Three of the other female workers decided to lock him in the ladies' loo. When I discovered this some time later, I went to rescue him. Not knowing who the women were who had tormented him, he assumed I had been the one responsible, and he reported me! The others never admitted it was them, and I received the admonition. I never forgave the three women.'

'I have a grudge against the girl at school who was given the lead in the school Christmas play for two consecutive years. Come on! She had rosebud lips and I still despise her forty-five years later with a passion!'

'I was turned down for a college course by a man who told me no woman with children had ever done the course. This rejection set me back – I didn't apply for a course again for about three years. (But then I went on a much better course and had a great time.) Years later, I ran into this man on the street. I had always promised myself I would punch him on the nose, but he turned out to be a puny little man and not worth the bother!'

'I have spent many years holding a grudge against a fellow professional who snubbed me at an event. I feel it has made me better at my job because I've felt it was necessary to prove myself better than him.'

'I'm an author and once I was told that I had thanked people in the wrong order on my acknowledgements page, the part of the book where I personally thank anyone who has helped me, or who I'm grateful to. I thanked a publicity assistant before a more senior publicity/marketing person, for which I received a supposedly helpful note from my editor saying, "Shouldn't you thank Annabel before Bev?" I'm a wimp, so I said, "Oh, yes, of course!" and made the change, but I was furious with the editor for trespassing on my acknowledgements page, the one and only page in any book that should be the author's, to do with as he/she wishes, and furious with myself for agreeing. I wish I'd said, "I'll thank people in whatever order I like, and anyone who bristles at being thanked after someone lower-ranking than themselves can just bugger off."'

'In 1994, my best friend came to stay with me and my boyfriend to comfort me the night before I was going to have an abortion. My boyfriend and I were no longer technically together, and the pregnancy was the result of a one-night stand. I woke up in the early hours needing the loo, only to hear the unmistakeable sounds of my ex and my bestie at it in the next room. Despite lines being crossed, we're still best friends; but she went out with my ex for a while and used to call me for advice on how to handle him. Oddly enough, this is the part I can't forgive her for.'

'My parents always told me I was fat when I was a child. I totally believed them, even though I was solidly built and not skinny, but certainly not fat. Then, as a young adult I started to put on weight and actually get fat, and it never occurred to me to try not to, because I wasn't worried about getting fat – after all, I was *already* fat as far as I believed, thanks to my parents. I blame them for making me think I didn't have a not-fat body that it was worth trying to maintain.'

'My friend Ginny used to say, nearly every time I saw her, "Ooh, I'd better not have a chocolate biscuit/cake — Richard's always told me he'll divorce me if I ever let my weight go over nine stone." I've no idea whether Richard would or wouldn't divorce her if she gained weight, though I suspect he wouldn't, but I can't believe that she doesn't realise how rude it is to keep saying this to me when she must know I weigh well over nine stone and am much heavier than her. What's wrong with just saying, "No, thanks, no cake for me!" and leaving it at that?'

'I got the commission I'd been waiting for all my life: I was asked to paint a portrait of a very famous politician, to be displayed at the National Portrait Gallery in London. I was thrilled about this. I was invited to the home of the politician in question and I met him and his wife and had dinner with them. Then, a few weeks after that, while I was watching

TV with my sister and her boyfriend, a programme came on about the politician I was going to paint. "Look," I said excitedly. "There he is! And his wife! I was in that room, I sat in that chair – that's their lounge!"

'My sister and her boyfriend ignored my excited splutterings, turned away from the screen (at exactly the same moment; they might almost have choreographed it) and picked up their phones. Then five minutes later, having not looked at the screen at all, they both stood up, yawned and said, "We're off to bed."'

'My father-in-law caused my wife to miss most of the dinner at her own wedding. Our oldest son was three months old when we got married and he was at the wedding hotel, in our room with a babysitter. My father-in-law is a terrible snob and wanted to show off to his brother and sister-in-law how smart the hotel was (that he wasn't paying for, although he didn't mention that!), so he took them on a tour, marching into everyone's rooms. When he marched into our room, our son woke up and became inconsolably and hysterically frightened. My wife had to leave the meal to calm him down. Now, however civil things are, I will never, never forgive him for how badly he treated my wife that day.'

'My husband and I were planning to spend the evening with our old friends Rob and Kelly. We'd left our son, Eddie, at my parents' house. They had agreed to babysit while we had our night out. We'd dropped Eddie off and were about to leave my parents' house and drive to Rob and Kelly's flat when I heard my mum say to Eddie, "Put your shoes back on. Your feet will get cold."

'I called out, "It's okay, Mum! He never wears shoes inside the house." My mother appeared in the hallway, looking displeased. "But his feet will get cold," she said. "Honestly, they won't." I told her. "It's July. It's warm. His feet never get cold – he never wears shoes at home. Only to go out." She didn't look happy, but she seemed to accept this. At least, she didn't argue any more.

'My husband and I drove to Kelly and Rob's place and were just pulling up outside when my mobile phone rang. It was my mother. I was surprised to hear from her, because we'd only just said goodbye to her and my dad. At that point in our lives, we saw my parents about once a fortnight. We had not seen Kelly and Rob for nearly a year. "Hi Mum," I said cheerfully. "What's up?" I wondered if maybe we'd left something at hers by mistake. "I'm furious with you," she said. Her voice was vibrating with rage.

'I was unaware of having done anything to enrage her, so I asked why she was angry. My husband frowned and pointed at the front door of the building where Rob and Kelly lived. I shrugged. How could I end this call, when my mum was furious with me? Our friends that we hadn't seen for ages would just have to wait. I remember feeling certain that sorting things out with my mum wouldn't take more than a few minutes.

'She proceeded to explain what I had done wrong, in her eyes. I'd told my son that he didn't have to put his shoes back on, after she'd said that he should. She said I had disrespected her by contradicting her. "In your own house, you and Eddie are free to do whatever you want," she said, "but you were in *my* house."

'My mother is someone who always wears her outdoor

shoes inside her house and everybody else's houses too. Unless she's in bed or getting ready for bed, she wears shoes. Even when watching TV in the lounge with a glass of sherry in her hand, her shoes are always on. "Mum," I said calmly. "I understand the principle of 'my house, my rules' but it surely doesn't apply to what one's guests choose to wear. It applies to things like 'No eating crumb-making snacks in the lounge' and 'no listening to loud heavy-metal at three in the morning'. If every time you came to my house, I asked you to wear a blonde curly Dolly Parton wig from the moment you crossed the threshold until the moment you left, would that be reasonable of me? Would you agree to do it?"

'One of my weird talents is that I am at my most effective and eloquent when being unreasonably attacked. (I think this might be because I've had so much practice!) I can lose my cool and act like a numbskull in almost any other situation, but never when being tyrannised in a way that's entirely preposterous.

'Unable to win the argument at the level of logic, my mother moved on to emotional blackmail: didn't I care about her happiness and what she wanted, when she'd been good enough to give up her evening to look after my child? I explained that of course I did, but that caring about someone's happiness and being grateful for their help did not mean that one ought to wear what that person wanted one to wear at all times. I suggested to my mum that she could make *herself* happier by deciding it was fine for Eddie to wander around with his shoes off.

'My husband, who had been sitting beside me in the car this whole time, signalled to me that we were now properly late. I told my mum that I really had to go – that Kelly and Rob were waiting for us – and that I would ring her the next day to continue the discussion of Eddie's shoes, if she really felt it needed to be continued. Her voice turned icy and she said, "Be very careful. Be *very* careful about what you do and say next." Without question, it was a threat.

'I was scared. I knew she would never hurt Eddie, but I hated the thought of him being in her care while she was in the frame of mind that made her sound this cold and evil. "Be careful of what?" I asked. "One day I'll be dead," said my mother. "And then you might regret insisting on this point of principle that means my grandson can't come to my house again."

'"*What*?" I said. "Are you saying that if I won't agree to make Eddie wear his shoes in your house, then he's not allowed to be in your house at all?" She sighed. "I would never say that my own grandson can't come to my house," she said. "But that's what you just implied," I said. "Or else, what did you mean? What are you threatening me with, exactly? I understand that one day you'll be dead, but if Eddie and I can continue to see you regularly for as long as you're alive, with or without shoes, then what's the problem?"

'My husband was rolling his eyes and shaking his head beside me as if to say, "What the fuck is going on?" I signalled to him that he should go on without me and have a nice evening with Kelly and Rob. There was no way I was going to have any fun tonight, I knew – not now that my mother had brought up the subject of her death. She'd had cancer; it was in remission at that point in time, but there was, in theory, a chance it could come back and kill her at any time. (About five years later it did. At no point since she passed

294

away have I regretted not allowing her to tyrannise or emotionally blackmail me on this occasion.)

'My husband left me to it and went inside. My mother asked if, on reflection, I would allow her to make Eddie put his shoes on. I said no, I wouldn't. She then launched into a tirade about how she was hoping not to have to say this (I love it when people say that!) but I had been acting for many years as if I didn't give a toss what she thought or how she felt about anything, and that this made her feel as if I didn't love her. I told her that I *did* love her, but that on occasions where she unreasonably tried to force me to do what she wanted, against my own wishes, I didn't allow myself to be pressurised in this way. I tried to explain to her that this was not the same thing as not loving her – not at all.

'By the time she was sounding normal and calm enough for me to feel safe leaving her to her own devices (and to continue looking after my son), two and a half hours had passed and I had missed a substantial chunk of my evening with Kelly and Rob. At the time, I remember feeling proud of myself for having stood up to my mother. Now, I feel very differently about this incident. I allowed her to steal most of my evening. I should have insisted on ending the phone call much, much earlier. I should have said, 'Sorry, Mum, I can't talk now. We'll have to discuss this another time.' If I didn't feel comfortable knowing that she was looking after Eddie while in a rage, I should have driven back to her house, collected Eddie and brought him to Rob and Kelly's house. If only I could turn back the clock, that is what I would do.'

'When our oldest child Finn was about a year old, my wife Jenny and I went on holiday with a guy we'd been at uni with and his wife. They had twin girls aged about nine months. On the first day, Jenny and our friends went off to put the kids to bed. We hadn't had any "grown-up time" yet, and I assumed that everyone would come back and we'd open a bottle of wine and have a chat and a proper catch-up. But while Jenny was still struggling with Finn, who wasn't good at getting off to sleep, our friends appeared downstairs in full tennis kit and carrying tennis rackets. "Do you mind keeping an eye on the girls while we go and have a game of tennis?" they asked, and of course I said it was fine. So for the next couple of hours, Jenny and I were left babysitting and making the supper. What really rankled was that there had been no discussion – they were already in their tennis kit and on their way out before they asked! All of a sudden, the holiday felt less like a nice opportunity to get together with our kids and have a catch-up, and more as if we were being used as handy babysitters while they went off and did what they wanted. We felt as if we were being taken for mugs, in a way. Not only have I slightly held this against that specific couple ever since, it's also become a transferable grudge – I have now a sort of proxy and unreasonable grudge against ALL friends who might wish me to go on holiday with them, and I refuse point blank to do so.'

'I was on maternity leave with my first baby and enjoying that time you never get again when a client who had a contract with us decided to break it. He justified the breaking of it with a completely spurious rationale – that he hadn't been happy with our performance for some time, that his product had been redeveloped now and he didn't want to risk it being handled by us because of this unhappiness. He'd never said a single word about dissatisfaction in quite a long relationship (in which we had worked hard to help him make the product the best it could be). It turned out that he had in fact developed an entirely new kind of product, and had already gone and sold it (though it was under contract to us) to another company who had had success with a product similar to his new product, for quite a lot more money.

'I would have been entirely happy if he had said to me that he knew he could get more money for this new product. We wouldn't have wanted to pay more so would have let it go with grace. I have always held a grudge about the fact that he pretended it was us that was at fault and interrupted my maternity leave to do it.'

'One Christmas a few years ago I was playing charades with a group of friends including my friend Lorena and her boyfriend Darran. I was on the same team as Darran and my own boyfriend Gerry. When Darran was acting out the charade, I kept shouting out the correct answer but he wouldn't hear me. It was like he was deaf to my voice only! My boyfriend Gerry noticed this, and started to shout out my answer after I'd said it. Darran would always hear him, and say "Yes, Gerry's got it!", after I had already guessed correctly first! I realised he had such low expectation of me guessing the correct answer that he had tuned me out. I exploded with rage and accused him of not hearing my voice because he didn't respect my opinion as a woman. We of course made up and are still good friends, in fact I was bridesmaid at Darran and Lorena's wedding. But I still feel that he doesn't take me seriously, and I'm always aware of it in conversations. Lorena has since confided that he often doesn't listen to her either, which confirmed my suspicions.'

'I've harboured a terrible grudge for many years towards a girl from school. While I was in the toilet, she tore up my beautifully coloured-in picture of Elmer the Elephant and threw it in the bin. We were around six years old at the time, so this is currently a twenty-year grudge!'

'I'm not sure if I can make anyone understand this particular grudge of mine. I've tried to explain to people why I hold a grudge about an apparently harmless action, but most people frown and go "So what?" when I tell them, and possibly think I'm mad. Maybe you will too. Here goes: I'm an author. A few years ago, for my birthday, my father gave me a framed 'Penguin Classic book cover' style poster, with my book on it – as if my book were a Penguin Classic. In fact, my debut novel had been published by a different publisher, not by Penguin.

'The whole joke/idea/point of a gift like that is, "Haha, let's pretend your book is a Penguin classic." I had written a novel, which was published by a publisher that's every bit as good as Penguin, and it sold pretty well. So, it didn't need or merit the patronising "Haha, let's pretend it's a Penguin classic" treatment. I was convinced that the true message of the gift was, "You might be published, but your book's no Penguin classic."

'My other objection to the poster was that I felt my father should surely have known that, in the publishing world, there are brands. These matter to publishers and authors. By giving me a poster portraying my book as a Penguin classic, my father was inaccurately and falsely branding my book. As

I said at the time, it's a bit like giving Alex Ferguson, longtime Manchester United manager, a mug saying "Alex Ferguson, Manager of Arsenal Football Club".'

'When my oldest son (now twenty-seven!) started school, there was another child (let's call him Graham) who was really horrible to everyone. He broke my son's new glasses three times in a week. The class teacher spoke to Graham's mum, who told me my son was "a wimp". She seemed to want me to agree with her, but instead she got a verbal tongue-lashing – I basically told her her son was a nasty thug. '"Twenty-seven years on, I still shudder at the name Graham and still wish very dire, horrible things on both him and his mother."'

'The first time I bought tickets to see Take That there were five band members but when the show came around there were four. So they owe me either £7.20 or one Robbie Williams show.'

'I am hugely tolerant but then once someone steps over the line, as far as I'm concerned, they're dead to me. I call it the Old Friend Graveyard. I have a dark mind, what can I say?

'Ex-boyfriend is the perfect example. I dated him for five years. He was a total narcissist, told me how amazing I was all the time, which I bought hook, line and sinker. When I gave up alcohol and wobbled emotionally he engineered it so that we broke up – he said that was clearly what I wanted. He carried on texting me his love for eight months and we would meet and have sex, until I found out he was seeing someone else and that's why he'd dumped me. My grudge for him knows no bounds, mostly built of fury with myself for being so badly duped by what I've since found out is a total con man. (I have zero issues with his new girlfriend.)'

'A regular visitor to my house occasionally tries to kill my dog. Well, not actively, perhaps. He doesn't strangle her or try to stab her, but he does things like accidentally leaving very cocoa-heavy chocolate lying around and "forgetting" to close the front door in the hope that the dog will run out onto the road and get run over. When this person is in my house, I watch my dog carefully at all times and hide the keys to my front door.'

'To the outside world my sister appears the nicest person but to family she is rude, aggressive and argumentative. We live in Australia so Christmas is in summer, and one year my sister was adamant that we were having Christmas on the beach. This meant travelling over an hour each way with my two kids (eighteen months and three and a half) but I agreed. On the day it was raining. Not an isolated shower, but rain that was forecast to stay around. I asked to change the venue but she refused and we stayed on the beach in the rain until the kids were moody, wet and not enjoying life. When I decided we would go home it was met with swearing, threats and me being told I was being selfish. I have not spoken to my sister in the almost three years since. I am happy with my grudge and I feel I am better for it.'

'In the run-up to Christmas one year, my domestic science class had to make and ice Christmas cakes. I'm not good at icing cakes, but I tried my very, very best. The cakes were put away in a cupboard for the icing to set and harden and, in the next lesson, the teacher pulled the cakes out of the cupboard one by one, asking whose they were. When she pulled mine out, she said, in front of the whole class, "And whose mess is this?" I can still feel my humiliation and anger to this day. Even though this was forty-six years ago and if she's still alive she'll be in her eighties, if I saw her I would cheerfully shove a custard pie in her face.'

'When I was seven, I had a metal tin where I kept my wax crayons. Once my dad put the tin on the radiator overnight because he didn't like it lying around. I even told him they'd melt but he said they wouldn't. And guess what – they did! I will never forget my melted crayons.'

'My huge galvanising grudge is directed towards my in-laws. When I learned that my husband was an alcoholic, at least partially due to a neglectful childhood, I immediately threw myself into researching and working on helping him with his recovery; his family on the other hand went into total denial. They never mentioned it when he visited, changed the subject if he brought it up and actually started trying to convince him that I was the problem. They said awful things about me – that I was worryingly and inappropriately possessive about our children and unwelcoming to them when they visited; they sent him messages trying to emotionally manipulate him into emotionally manipulating me (what a sentence!), which upset him so much he ended up relapsing.

'I made a final attempt to set fair boundaries with them, but ultimately they didn't want to budge and when his sisters became aggressive I decided to go no-contact. I haven't seen them for years now.

'I would have been perfectly willing to let go of my animosity toward his family had they been willing to stop with the guilt trips. But that will never happen, so I tend to my fury instead. I feel desperately sad for that little boy my husband once was, who was taught that nobody cared about his feelings and that he was unworthy of love and belonging. I think of my grudge as appropriate accountability and it honestly helps.'

(Author's note: I saved this last grudge up so that it could be the very last 'Other People's Grudges' grudge in the book. I love that last line. Our good grudges are exactly that: appropriate accountability; a small measure of private justice.)

The Grudge-fold Path Quiz

'Forgive your enemies, but never forget their names.'

John F Kennedy

Think back to the quiz you took all those pages ago, when you first started reading this book. You know *so* much more about grudge-holding now than you did then, so I wanted to give you another quiz to round things off, and so that you can assess the extent to which your thinking about grudges has changed now that you've all been introduced to the Grudge-fold Path.

1. Someone who has always interfered with your work previously is so impressed by one thing you did, they perform a very visible supportive act. Do you:

a) still not trust them – remember all those unsupportive things they did? They still matter.

b) adopt new attitude and cancel the grudge.

c) feel confused. Do they like your work or not?

2. You hear that a teacher has accused your child of something she didn't do. The same teacher has also (in your child's absence) told her class that your child has a poor work ethic (which isn't true). School believed her, not the teacher, and she wasn't punished. She's leaving at the end of this term, anyway. Do you:

a) forget all about it – no harm was done as your daughter wasn't punished and the teacher is leaving anyway.

b) challenge the teacher in a polite way – ask her why she is behaving in this way, because it feels to you as if she's being very unfair to your daughter.

c) hold a grudge against the teacher and bitch about her with your daughter, so your daughter sees you're on her side.

3. Your friend tells you that she's just been offered the job of her dreams. You didn't even know she'd applied and you're hurt because you tell her everything. She says she didn't tell you because if she didn't get it, she'd have been embarrassed to fail publicly. Do you:

a) hold a grudge because you'd have told her if you were doing the same.

b) hold no grudge, understand her motivation and congratulate her – no hard feelings.

c) congratulate her, but re-evaluate whether you want to tell her everything quite as much as you did before.

4. Your mother has a new boyfriend. She makes a point of telling all your siblings about him, but not you. Then later she says to you, 'I expect you've heard about Jim! I'd love you to meet him.'

Do you:

a) count this as her telling you about Jim, so all is now fine – she's told you, just like she told the siblings.

b) decide that all is not fine. She relied on them telling you. Hold grudge based on unequal treatment that suggests you can just 'find out' whereas the others deserve to be told. Say, 'Yes, I've heard about Jim – I'd love to meet him' or not depending on whether you would. Remember you might need to protect yourself emotionally from a parent who treats her children so unequally.

c) say something like, 'Who's Jim? Never heard of him. If you want me to know about him, you'd better tell me.'

5. Every time you talk to your friend Sheila on the phone about something that matters to you, she puts a time limit on the conversation. She always has to go after ten or fifteen minutes to deal with work/kids/dog/husband/volunteering. Sheila is one of the busiest people you know, but you are just as busy as she is, and you – when she needs you to talk to her at length about her issues – will cancel things if necessary, or get up earlier, or stay up later, to give her unlimited attention. Do you:

a) ditch her and find a new friend, because she's clearly a selfish bitch.

b) continue the friendship, continue to like her, but hold a 'failure of reciprocity' grudge – remember Sheila will not give you as much as you have always wanted to give her – and adjust your willingness to give her your time accordingly. Since you are busy too, do you really want to make top priority someone who doesn't do that for you?

c) hold no grudge – if you give your time and attention freely, you shouldn't expect anything back. It's up to her to decide how long she wants to talk to you for.

6. Someone tells you you shouldn't hold the grudge you're holding against Mark because it's bad for you, and also he'd see the situation differently. Do you:

a) say, actually grudges are *good for me*, and here's why – then explain everything you've learned in this book about the Grudge-fold Path.

b) hold a grudge against the person who said it for, because it's not okay for him to tell you how to feel and think about your own experience, but be willing to cancel that grudge completely if that person ever says to you, 'Oh, my God! I'm *so* sorry I said that. It was completely out of order.'

c) say nothing, because what's the point? But hold a grudge against the person who said it for being wrong.

7. Someone tells you to talk it out with the person you have the grudge against, instead of holding something against them secretly. They accuse you of being two-faced. Do you:

a) tell them that your grudge is *about* somebody but not *against* somebody, and that you're under no obligation to be honest and revelatory about how you think/feel. It's fine for you to think what you want, even something negative, while continuing to be friendly, as long as you don't actively lie and say 'You're my favourite person ever'.

b) If that grudge-in-place friendliness from you leads to good behaviour on their part that leads to you deciding to cancel the grudge, then great! If not, then the relationship can't be improved from your point of view, as it is fundamentally flawed, so why the obligation to communicate 100 per cent honestly?

c) ask the person if they would advise you to take off your bulletproof vest before going to a meeting with someone who's going to be armed with three guns, and who's shot at you many times before? If they say no, explain to them that your grudge is protection in a very similar way.

d) all of the above.

QUIZ ANSWERS

The correct answer is b) for every question except the last one, for which the correct answer is d). If you didn't get them all right, don't worry, and don't hold a Selfie Grudge. After all, you've only just finished reading this book, and it takes a while for Grudge-fold Path wisdom to become second nature. Keep following the Grudge-fold path and all will be well! If you want to ask me why the answer/s you've chosen are wrong because you don't see how they can be, email me at grudgescanbegood@gmail.com and I will be very happy to discuss it with you.

Before I go, I have one last little story for you. Once, on a Greek ferry, I met a guru. I told him about my grudge habit and my strong desire for justice and he said, 'Trust me: nobody gets away with anything.' At the time, I thought, 'Are you crazy, mate?' but now I know exactly what he meant, and I agree with him. I know a man called Lancelot (come on, it's my last made-up name – let me be a bit extravagant!) who chose to support something terrible when he could so easily have chosen differently. He might not be in prison or exiled to Siberia, but the poor choice he made was noticed, and, as a direct result, he has missed out on so many treats and wonderful things that he could have had if only he had made a more ethical choice.

Compare and contrast Lancelot's situation with that of Zelda, who behaved so kindly and with such ethical soundness that many of her acquaintances were eager to offer her opportunities, gifts and help that they would never have offered if she hadn't so clearly been a force for good.

My personal experience supports this theory. (Scientists: stop thinking 'She can't prove...' I know I can't. It's just a theory. Relax.) Whenever I do or say a petty or mean-spirited thing, I get zapped by suffering almost immediately. The opposite is also true: when I do something kind or good, or resist a dishonourable impulse, something wonderful tends to happen to me soon afterwards.

This is good news for us followers of The Grudge-fold Path (I'm going to assume a few of you have joined me by now). Why? Because it means that the world — or what spiritual types call 'the universe' — is a follower of that same path. Don't take my word for it — practice following The Grudge-fold Path and you'll soon start to see evidence that Someone-or-Something Up There is smiling down approvingly at your Grudge Cabinet and at all the grudges carefully folded inside it.

If you're keen to delve into the subject of grudges with me in more detail and hear more jaw-dropping grudge stories, you might want to listen to my brand new podcast, which has the same title as this book – *How To Hold A Grudge* – and is completely free to download. See you there! And in the meantime . . .

Grudge safely, my friends, and grudge well!

Helen Acton is a BACP- and UKCP-registered existential psychotherapist in private practice in Cambridge, and on staff at Trinity College, University of Cambridge.

Anne Grey is a practitioner of Emotional Freedom Therapy, a fellow of The Healer Foundation and a council member of the BCMA. Throughout her therapeutic practice she has offered mentoring and training, and she has been a teacher of ascension meditation for the last ten years. Anne is currently writing a book – *The Grace and Ease of Now – Release the Past, Take the Fear Out of The Future* – that will bring together what she has learned from her therapeutic practice and her meditation practice.